gardens of the

FRENCH RIVIERA

LOUISA JONES

PHOTOGRAPHY BY VINCENT MOTTE

Flammarion

Designed by Marc Walter
Copyediting by Christa Weil
Typesetting by Octavo Editions, Paris
Photoengraving by Colourscan, France
Printed and bound in Italy by Canale, Turin

All photographs in this book are by Vincent Motte except those on the following pages by Louisa Jones: 12, 13, 17 (above), 25, 34 (both photos), 39 (below), 56, 64 (above), 65, 106 (left), 112, 113, 126, 127, 130 (below), 152 (both photos), 177 and 178.

ISBN: 2-0801-0717-8
FA 0717-02-II
Dépôt légal: 04/2002

Flammarion
26, rue Racine
75006 Paris, France

To all the new friends encountered while preparing this book and to my oldest friend, my husband.

CONTENTS

THE GOLDEN RIVIERA

The
riant bloom of
ainvillea or "paper
r" decks villas and
ens all along
Riviera. This genus
rising fourteen
es and many
d varieties
nated in tropical
America (page 1).
riance and
cism mark many
ra gardens:
palms, oleanders,
eucrium each
ibute to this vivid
ay (pages 2-3).
sea limits,
nues, prolongs,
bles, enchants this
luminous
line. . . ." Thus
te described such
atic Riviera
apes
es 4-5). The first
Riviera gardens
up on rocky
ontories jutting out
he Mediterranean,
e picturesque
frame the wine-
sea (pages 6-7).

The French Riviera stretches for some two hundred miles between Provence and Italy; if it shares with these two neighbors an ancient Mediterranean heritage, the strip of narrow coastline between Hyères and Menton has known a special destiny unique in Europe. An unusual blending of climate, topography, and cultural layering has produced a fantastic land of wish fulfillment, a playground for princes and a paradise for plant collectors since the eighteenth century. "Côte d'Azur," the name invented by poet Stéphane Liégeard in 1887, conjures up not only the wine-dark inland sea but a world where the most desirable visions of beauty could be realized. The very word "azur" evoked such an ideal for the entire French Symbolist generation, of which Liégeard was part.

A particularly privileged climate first drew the cosmopolitan elite to this idyllic realm. Mountains rising immediately behind the sea protect its well-exposed coastline, producing a mixture of sea and sun by now famous the world over. Reality is more complex than the blue and gold travel poster, however. On the one hand, the French Riviera contains in its narrow band several different geological formations—the purple, porphyry crests and inlets of the Estérel mountains, the limestone ridges of the Maures range among them. On the other, the region offers a broad range of climatic variations: near Hyères, around Beaulieu in the area called "Little Africa," or in the Garavan Bay of Menton, for example, are sheltered, south-facing hillsides where temperatures rarely drop below freezing. In the backcountry, however, the winter thermometer can register -10° centigrade. This combined wealth of soil types and exposures has long tempted botanists and collectors eager to test the limits of the land, to grow ever new plant varieties and to realize their own particular dreams impossible elsewhere. Today, these havens with their special microclimates continue to display a riot of colorful exotic treasures. All combinations of local, Mediterranean, and imported vegetation can now be found in happy profusion, for the greater delight of gardeners, whether they be world-famous collectors or the recently retired owners of small backyard plots. This plant variety adds a texture and brilliance to the French Riviera which is quite distinctive.

Mountains crowding the sea, rising steeply from the littoral, also offer design possibilities unlike those elsewhere in France. Contemporary gardeners farther west in Provence can choose to settle in the fertile, agricultural plains of the Alpilles or the Comtat, around old châteaux or valley farms, or else in renovated village houses. Few undertake the cost of restoring steep hillsides, layered with stone retaining walls supporting miles of terracing, when so many easier solutions are available.

On the French Riviera, the options are quite different. The first great gardens were made on the famous "caps," or rocky promontories, jutting out into the sea near Antibes, Nice, Monaco and Menton, by owners willing to undertake major earthworks and bring in small mountains of topsoil. Contemporary gardeners generally prefer the steep, terraced slopes of former olive plantations in the backcountry. Almost all have lovingly framed a view of the Mediterranean in the distance. Mountain and sea have a special, magic intimacy on the Côte d'Azur, generally not traditional in Provence, but fostered here by their dramatic proximity.

Riviera hillsides possess the oldest olive trees in France, spared during the killing frosts of 1956 and 1985 by the milder climate of this region. As in Italy, these giants have fully developed the ancient, gnarled, sculptural forms coveted by every contemporary gardener, not simply as a décor but as friends full of character and ever-changing moods. Above all, the caprices of history have filled these sites with endless kilometers of jasmine, roses, myrtle, wisteria, tuberose, and citrus of all kinds. This wealth of fragrance burgeoned over the past five centuries thanks to the perfume industry which thrived in Grasse. While other Mediterranean regions were struggling to survive on chick peas, olives, grapes, and almonds, the French Riviera was already producing mountains of flowers.

THE CULTURAL KALEIDOSCOPE

The perfumeries of Grasse initiated a peculiarly cosmopolitan expansion of this essentially rural region, a development which

The
Hanbury Botanical
Gardens, east of
Menton, seen through
the arches of the Villa
Orengo (center).

Maupassant
described the Estérel
Inlets as "elegantly
sculpted, with coquetry
and yet artistically."
A famous couturière
has transformed such
a site into imaginative
gardens (preceding page).

intensified considerably at the end of the eighteenth century and even more during the Romantic period. Nature had been kind to start with; human ingenuity would prove boundless. Bit by bit, the fabulous phenomenon of the French Riviera came into being.

Henry, Lord Brougham, lord chancellor of England, is generally credited with its "invention." In 1834, tired after years of fighting for the abolition of the slave trade, the reduction of illiteracy, and a long list of other liberal causes, he came south for his health and that of a sickly daughter. Before reaching Nice, his party was turned back because of a cholera epidemic and was obliged to take refuge in a hotel near Cannes. Lord Brougham so fell in love with the place that he bought land nearby, constructing an Italianate mansion which he named after his daughter: the Villa Eléonore. Stendhal saw it soon after and deemed it "a pretty little château." It was surrounded by extensive lawns, astoundingly green all winter long. For at this stage of the Riviera's evolution, no one, not even an Englishman, was mad enough to consider spending summers on this coast. Designer Roderick Cameron, writing in the 1960s, could still remember how

in days gone by, in late spring, "the gardens, along with the house, were put away, disappeared as it were under dust sheets. Heavy and clayey, the soil hardened and cracked, lawns were dug up. . . . Even the gravel paths vanished, were scraped to one side ready for autumn. . . ."

The winter season was brilliant, however. Many distinguished Englishmen followed the lord chancellor's example, establishing elaborately landscaped properties. Among them, Thomas Robinson Woolfield began building and selling to his friends. He, too, was a man of many parts: a pious believer instrumental in establishing the first Anglican church on the coast, a landscaper whose lawns were so perfect that Queen Victoria played croquet on them, a plantsman credited with introducing the eucalyptus to the Riviera. His gardens were laid out by one John Taylor, who also launched into real estate, so successfully that one of his descendants continues the business in Cannes to this day.

Many of these nineteenth-century domains still survive precariously like the fabulous froth of a long-gone golden age. And Lord Brougham is honored by a statue in the heart of Cannes, which commends him for marrying the palm

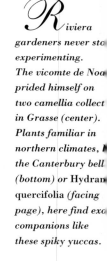

Riviera gardeners never sto[p] experimenting. The vicomte de Noa[illes] prided himself on two camellia collect[ions] in Grasse (center). Plants familiar in northern climates, [like] the Canterbury bell[s] (bottom) or Hydran[gea] quercifolia (facing page), here find exo[tic] companions like these spiky yuccas.

tree with the rose of England. Not everyone approved of his influence: Prosper Mérimée, then inspector for the French ministry of historical monuments, protested vehemently that these English "cardboard castles" were so many blots on the landscape, like "paper flowers in the midst of a parterre."

The French Riviera, it has been said, was a British invention, a sort of benevolent cultural invasion which completely transformed the localities it touched. This is reflected in the title of Patrick Howarth's amusing account of English presence in this region: *When the Riviera Was Ours.* But Lord Brougham and his cronies were not the only worldly, highly traveled men with an interest in plants and gardens. Historians Michel Racine and Ernest Boursier-Mougenot list several elaborate botanical gardens predating Brougham's arrival in the area. Not least were the exotic collections donated by the empress Josephine in 1804 to the administrator of the gardens of Nice, plants which had been cultivated in the glasshouses at Malmaison but which here could survive outdoors.

French journalist, writer, and drama critic Alphonse Karr arrived in the 1860s, soon after the building of the railroad which allowed him to start sending cut flowers up to Paris for sale in the markets. He opened a flower shop in Nice, a simple eccentricity for a successful man of letters, but he counted among his customers the crowned heads of Europe. He was known for his Parisian wit: it is said that Karr once asked to consult rare botanical books belonging to his neighbor, the king of Sweden, who agreed on condition they be examined in his own library. Some time after, the king asked to borrow Karr's watering cans, and the Parisian readily agreed, provided they be used on his own property. . . .

In 1864, Karr settled in Saint-Raphaël, where his villa was characteristically called the Maison Close. It is said that he would draw the shutters on sight of unwanted visitors. He was, however, willing to receive the likes of Dumas *fils*, Maupassant, Gounod, and Berlioz. Karr was devoted to his garden, which grew beautifully, and his commendation of it has often been quoted: "Come plant your walking stick in my garden, the next day when you awake you will find that it has sprouted roses."

English and Parisian: these two influences certainly contributed early on to the French Riviera legend, supported by many lesser strains—in the 1920s, it was the Americans who initiated the fashion for a summer season. Opulence and extravagance were the essence from the start. Even those who claimed to be fleeing the world and its pomp did so very publicly. Karr's gesture with the shutters, like his mode of dress (in black, followed by a black labrador and a mulatto servant garbed all in red), was above all theatrical. Exiles, escapists, and pleasure-seekers of all description created flamboyant new stages for extravagant display. Gambling flourished as the railroad, and later the automobile, made the pursuit of fleeting moments of pleasure even more accessible. The Casino in Monte-Carlo became a new Mecca for dubious pilgrims. The Côte d'Azur, after all, offered forbidden fruits as well as flowers: this was the home of permissiveness, which British novelist Somerset Maugham called "a sunny place for shady people."

The region quickly evolved into a land of wish fulfillment created by, and for, a select group of people who could afford any whim. Where else could American press magnate James Gordon Bennett, unable to find a seat in his favorite restaurant in Monte-Carlo, buy the establishment on the spot and give the deed as a tip to the fortunate and astonished waiter?

The French Riviera was first created by a social as well as financial elite which included many crowned heads. But it was not only a worldly phenomenon: in both the Belle Epoque and between the world wars, Europe's artistic leaders also flocked to the Côte d'Azur in pursuit of their own visions of idyllic sunshine. The desires of all these people, generation after generation, were infinite, varied, and unpredictable: sometimes surrealistic, at times vulgar, almost always festive and showy. A good number of these desires took shape as gardens.

It must be said that there was also an indigenous gardening heritage, difficult now to untangle from the cosmopolitan overlay. In early times, a certain number of private domains were even open to the public, perhaps more than today. As of the late eighteenth century, travel guides regularly described the elegant parks of local gentry,

he Menton gardens of Maria Serena, set around a "wedding cake" Belle Epoque villa, contain a celebrated collection of palm trees (center).

Prolific Acacia dealbata, commonly called mimosa, spreads its golden profusion on slopes around the village of Bormes in the Var region (following pages).

Eighteenth-century travelers like novelist Tobias Smollett admired the intermingling of flowers, vegetables, and fruit in Riviera gardens—at that time usually roses, sweet William, peas, anemones, lettuces, and citrus. Collectors today can choose from a much broader spectrum, including Abutilon x milleri *(above) and the exquisite* Campanula takeïsmenia *(center).*

such as the handsome villa of Count Gubernatis at Cimiez, which now houses the Archaeological Museum of Nice. A certain Miss Brewster, writing in the nineteenth century, admired the Villa Arson of Doctor Arnulfi, where Talleyrand stayed and British novelist Lord Lytton wrote one of his books. Italianate garden walks lined with statues, grottoes, and staircases and a famous collection of camellias made this property "one of the fashionable sights of the fashionable world of Nice." If the Côte d'Azur legend was created by foreigners (including Parisians), all historians record examples of a strong local interest in plants and gardens which not only predates the arrival of the English but goes back hundreds of years.

With their formal parks and centuries-old trees, a number of distinguished family properties still bear witness to this heritage. Grouped mostly on the hills behind Nice, the region's major city, or around Grasse, center of the perfume industry, their style evokes Italy—just as Niçois cooking resembles that of Genoa. Thus the Villa Châteauneuf in the hills above Nice contains a seventeenth-century courtyard with a series of arcades around a formal parterre, each sheltering the bust of a different caesar. An inscription

dated 1681, a madrigal in Piedmontese, celebrates the charms of Flora. This property is still in the hands of the family for whom it was built, although much of the once extensive park has recently gone to developers.

Similarly, the eighteenth-century Villa d'Andon near Grasse displays, on its series of terraces, an elegant descent with basins and fountains, canopies of ancient planes sheltering the main façade (with one of the region's most exuberant wisterias), a formal box walk leading to the statue of a faun, all in a symphony of soft ochers and greens—a fine, authentic survivor.

As the Côte d'Azur became fashionable, English arrivals often bought up and then transformed such old properties. At the Villa Garibondy, during the Belle Epoque, the prestigious Paget family regularly received Queen Victoria, who deigned to plant a parasol pine in their sumptuous lawn in 1891. The Paget roses were famous—but there were no palms in spite of prevailing trends. Today the domain survives, an unsuspected haven near Cannes, a marriage of two cultures.

Indigenous tradition, long overshadowed by the mythmakers, has recently come to the fore once more as part of the contemporary vogue. Today's cosmopolitan sophisticate,

uchsia
...s and Salvia
...ntha (above) can
...und at the
...zaro nurseries.
...humble zucchini
...r (center) now
...ars on the best
...s of the region.

who still comes to the French Riviera to realize personal fancies, puts a premium on rural roots, turning country style into an elegant "art of living."

LEMONS AND PALMS, CYPRESSES AND OLIVE TREES

Riviera dreams, and the gardens they produced, have followed a series of fashions since the eighteenth century, each symbolized by a particular tree. In the beginning, it was the citrus family which beckoned to northern travelers. The year-round, bright green foliage of these trees came to symbolize the magical presence of summer in winter, or of eternal spring and another impossible dream fulfilled. Madame de Sévigné exclaimed on the wonderful oranges, oleanders, and pomegranates she saw in Nice, and historians Racine and Boursier-Mougenot go so far as to claim that "the introduction of the orange tree in the region marks the birth of the oldest gardens known there." Goethe, of course, sent generations southward with his famous line about "the land where the lemon tree blooms."

The citrus family embodies the whole early history of the French Riviera, its unique climatic possibilities, and its industries—both perfume and agriculture. In homage to its versatility, the town of Menton holds a lemon festival every February. This small, picturesque community near the Italian border possesses such a mild climate that lemon trees here produce flowers and fruit at all stages of development all year round, a growth habit impossible elsewhere north of Palermo. Menton is so proud of this fact that it has created a municipal park around the Palais Carnolès to display the wide range of citrus varieties which here grow outdoors.

A colorful Menton legend honors the magic lemon tree. One version was told by a washerwoman of Garavan to English tourist Frances M. Gostling in 1927: "As Eve sadly followed her husband to the Gate of Paradise, she stopped and plucked a bough of lemons. 'They will serve to remind us of our dear first home,' said she, 'and, besides, lemons are so refreshing when one is travelling.' The couple wandered unhappily until chance brought them to the site of Menton. Here Eve exclaimed, 'Look, we have found it at last—our second Paradise.' It is still Paradise," adds Mrs. Gostling, "the most beautiful spot on all the Riviera, a place of palms and whispering waves, golden sunsets, dreams, and fairy tales!"

Mrs. Gostling's "palms and whispering waves" recall the late-nineteenth-century

ardens
today benefit from generations of preceding fashions: olive trees flanked by palms, oleanders, autumn-gold wisteria, and Beschorneria yuccoides surround a mountain swimming pool (following pages).

fashion for exoticism, when palm trees came to reign on the Côte d'Azur. Although observed already near Hyères in the sixteenth and seventeenth centuries, their introduction is widely cited as occuring anywhere from 1830 to 1870. The Canary Island date palm, *Phoenix canariensis*, is said to have been acclimatized first by the comte de Vigier in Nice in 1864, spreading soon after westward along the coast and becoming in particular the totem tree of the city of Hyères. Palms of all varieties compelled the imagination toward exotic reveries. Flaubert, listening to the wind rustle in the fronds in Toulon, surrounded by fragrant flowers whose names he did not know, felt his "heart grow weak, all ready to love."

"A rising-up against the tyranny of the potted plant; for tyranny it had become when a gardener could boast of using 350,000 pots in one season! Gone are the parti-coloured mounds of cinerarias and cyclamens, the mosaic borders and single palms set in primulas; the more trained and intelligent love of gardening, developed in recent years in England and America, would no longer tolerate this lifeless form of decoration, even if the increased cost of labour did not make it impossible. The cypresses of the country replace the foreign palm; and great masses of rock plants, flowering shrubs, mimosa (*acacia*) and climbing

With their fabulous collec of exotic plants at La Mortola, the Hanbury brothers u always the forerun of fashion, never its followers (facing pa

Citrus trees appeal for their fresh, year-round foliage, perfumed flowers, and fruit like golden lanterns (center).

Palm trees on tourist brochures from towns all along the coast still make people dream. In most cases, however, the planting on the Riviera was not evocative of jungle settings or uncharted tropical islands. Rather the trees took their place, as they do today, in semiformal landscaped layouts, as avenues or stands, their feet encircled by the geometries of bright bedding plants. Even private exotic gardens often had the look of a public park, such as those still seen around the Casino in Monaco today.

The early twentieth century witnessed another important shift in sensibilities. Garden chronicler Mrs. Martineau wrote a book in 1924 called *Gardening in Sunny Lands* in which she disdained the old style and triumphantly proclaimed the new, as:

plants have superseded the elaborate 'bedding out' of the old school."

The cypress indeed did now hold sway, not only in gardens influenced by the new horticultural movement in England, but also in the fashionable rehabilitation of southern styles. Artist and designer Ferdinand Bac united both cypress and olive trees in gardens evoking a full range of Mediterranean myths.

Italian models were much admired and imitated in the grand parterres created by English landscaper Harold Peto, as well as French architects and garden designers Achille Duchêne, Octave Godard, Jean Claude Nicolas Forestier, and many others up and down the coast.

Today, the olive tree is the undisputed sovereign. Gardeners and landscapers once again stress ties with Provence and Italy, their common Mediterranean heritage re-emerging. It has endured with surprising persistence. After all, national and regional boundaries imposed somewhat arbitrary divisions on a land which, since ancient times, made its living from the grazing of sheep and goats, the culture of the vine, olive, and fruit trees. There are still peasants in the hills behind Nice, in spite of the pressure of promoters hoping to buy up their land. Some peasants can still be found selling their produce at the wholesale market, speeding down the motorway from their mountain farms and back again. Contemporary opinion now

created in one small area—still more so now, when there is no longer a specific winter or summer season. Gardens must be beautiful all year round, an even greater challenge than those faced by earlier generations. To this end, imagination is as important a driving force as wealth. Not all of today's gardens are realized thanks to colossal fortunes and extravagant expenditure. Some of the most ingenious recently created gardens on the French Riviera are modest in their means and surface area. Indeed, contemporary gardening here reserves many surprises, some of which will be revealed in the following chapters. Many of the historical properties are widely celebrated, of course, those which helped create the Riviera myth from the

Elaborate formal gardens at the Villa Fiesole in Cannes were created in the 1920s by the painter Jean-Gabriel Domergue and sculptor Odette Maujendre-Villiers (whose works still provide much of its elegant décor). Brilliant receptions are sponsored here today by the city of Cannes (center).

regards their traditional regimen as a model for the healthy, simple life. Virgil had already said as much. . . .

At the same time, today's gardens perpetuate the practice, constant since the invention of the Riviera, of picking and choosing from each epoch as from each part of the world exactly those elements which best suit each owner's individual dream. Regional style on the Côte d'Azur can mean only this infinite variety of personal dreams, made possible by a permissive climate and a brilliantly varied history. The Riviera mode is fanciful and fabulous, always pushing back the limits of reality in one direction or another. Anything goes, and everything does.

Nowhere else in the world, perhaps, has such a great range of extravagant visions been

Belle Epoque to the postwar period and have greatly influenced all later creations. These now constitute the region's rich garden heritage. Some are open to the public, others will be so after sadly needed restoration. The tale of their elaboration, their rise (and, in some cases, fall) conjures up the whole golden myth once again.

A number of these gardens were set on terraced hillsides—as indeed the great majority of Côte d'Azur properties both old and new must be, given the topography of the region. The importance of this common situation is generally overlooked, yet nothing reveals more fully the amazing variety of French Riviera creations than a sampling of the uses to which the classic terraced hillside can be put. Now that backcountry gardening

Judas trees and flowering cherries grace old Provençal gardens, enhanced on the Ri[viera] by palms and eucaly[ptus] (facing page).

leads contemporary fashion, the versatility of such locations counts more than ever.

Similarly, because the legendary domains were so opulent, little attention has been paid to the Côte d'Azur's intimate gardens, some evolving from the English horticultural tradition, others resulting from the efforts of modest but passionate plantsmen.

Grand gardens still exist today, however, many quite deliberately theatrical in their design. Some of those still in their prime have old roots, but, having always shunned the limelight of their more celebrated contemporaries, still remain extremely private and exclusive. Others are entirely recent creations, drawing on the wealth of past models and the equally stimulating riches of newly available plants to renew the grand tradition of the Riviera show garden.

A region so rich in whimsy and imagination provides near-infinite variety. Other themes in Côte d'Azur gardening

could be envisaged, and these are not mutually exclusive. But these particular choices permit a fresh look at a jaded, much overrun region, and the inclusion of many as yet unknown and fascinating examples.

The two great tendencies which seem to dominate the garden world generally, the design bias and the passion for plant collecting, intermingle in all these types of Riviera garden, from the most intimate to the most grand. But there too, the combinations are sometimes quite surprising.

The French Riviera has left behind its images of elitist extravagance, and of sea-and-sun vacation glamour, and is now moving toward a mode of quiet elegance. Gardens play an important part in this new Côte d'Azur, many clinging to backcountry hillsides and the rural traditions they embody, some small, lush, and highly textured, others essentially theatrical, designed for a whole new show. And the curtain is only just rising.

*M*any *Belle Epoque* *ns framed* *co's long spur, as* *t the Villa* *ebrune,* *rlining thus the* *nt contrast* *en their own* *sion and the* *ipality's worldly* *e (facing page).*

*C*ycas revoluta, *from coastal Japan, flowers here in the gardens of Villa Maria Serena (Menton). This species already existed one hundred million years ago (center).*
Les Cèdres, private botanical gardens, contain such wonders as this brilliant Caesalpina japonica syn. sepiara, too rampant and thorny for most smaller gardens (following pages).

LEGENDARY
GARDENS

Many fabulous properties have survived from the golden age of the French Riviera, though one cannot help marveling at all that has disappeared. One should indeed say "golden ages," for there were successive periods of legendary garden-making: from the Renaissance through the seventeenth and eighteenth centuries, aristocratic domains were laid out for old families; in the nineteenth century, English whimsies, international exotic collections, and landscaped parks proliferated; after World War I, there were the twin movements toward Mediterranean formality, on the one hand, and English horticulture on the other. Many different types of people have gardened on the French Riviera for many different reasons. The gardens described in this chapter were created from the Victorian era to the period just after World War II. All were—and are—highly celebrated. All have exerted tremendous influence as models, sometimes through several generations. These are all opulent gardens, extravagant expressions of talented and privileged owners. Spurred by their common interest, many of them knew each other, trading plants, advice, and discoveries with great generosity. Some are still present in tombs or mausoleums on the grounds they transformed, a gesture to grandeur few contemporary owners would dare to contemplate or care to imitate.

Many of these properties are now open to the public, a few are undergoing restoration, and many more worthy domains stand in dire need. Taken all together, the grand gardens of the Riviera represent a cultural heritage perhaps unique in the world, whose preservation is devoutly to be wished. But even the most derelict among them persist as legends, and enchant to this very day.

LA MORTOLA

The greatest of Riviera gardens must be La Mortola—great in its accumulated years, the richness of its collections, the power of its presence on all who behold it, and, not least, in the impact it has had all over the French Riviera. Although, in fact, La Mortola lies just beyond the Italian border, eight kilometers west of Ventimiglia. The tale of its origins

has often been told: how in 1867, Thomas Hanbury, a prosperous British merchant, spotted from a rowboat at sea this terraced hillside, its dense groves of citrus, vines, olives, and cypresses surrounding the ruins of the Renaissance-era Villa Orengo. He imagined there a great experimental garden. The microclimate and soil composition of this spot proved conducive to the culture of rare exotics from all over the world, the northernmost limit for a certain number of African species including the papyrus. Thomas enlisted the aid of his brother Daniel, renowned botanist and pharmacologist, and the garden soon achieved fame, thanks in part to the generosity of the Hanburys, who welcomed public interest and worldwide exchanges. So much so that in 1937, 18,000 packages of seeds were sent to collectors abroad.

By then, of course, Sir Thomas's son Cecil had taken over the property, aided by a series of distinguished German curators. Cecil's wife Dorothy and her brother Bertram Symons-Jeune introduced notions of garden design to the fabulous collections, creating vistas, pergolas, belvederes, fountains, and a small temple. The garden gained at this time its single, dramatic axis down the hillside, with its landings, curved steps, grottoes, and pools.

Dorothy Hanbury's contributions, qualities, and limitations have been somewhat controversial, but much credit must be given her for restoring the garden, with reduced means, after World War II. It had served for war games and battle maneuvers, been bombed by all armies, witnessed a secret meeting between Mussolini and Franco in 1941, had its invaluable library and seed collections dispersed to the winds, and been heavily mined, as were most coastal gardens at the time. Dorothy sold the property to the Italian government and many years passed while the exact nature of its administration was settled. Today, the newly named Hanbury Botanical Gardens are administered by Professors Paola Profumo and Paola Gastaldo of the Botanical Institute of the University of Genoa, a body which was founded in part thanks to Sir Thomas's contribution of land in 1892. They are seconded by curator Dr. Campadonico and an advisory committee of international experts.

The Hanburys always welcomed the public

The particularly sheltered hills above Menton's bay of Garavan hosted some of the Belle Époque's most fantastic gardens, a unique heritage for this picturesque city (facing page).

The Hanbury brothers not only grew beautiful yucca flowers at La Mortola but introduced just the right insect to pollinate them (center).

The Hanbury gardens around the Villa Orengo spread luxuriantly above the blue sheet of the Mediterranean. Versatile, blue-flowered Teucrium fruticans often serves as hedging (following pages).

and willingly served as a conduit for worldwide exchanges of information and plants. The current administration renews this tradition. Plants are again carefully labeled, and are maintained by fifteen gardeners. A trained, youthful staff receives the 50,000 visitors who come yearly. Detailed records will again be maintained as they were for many decades, including a yearly list established of plant varieties. On one occasion, as many as four hundred plant species and varieties were found to be flowering on January 1! A recent television documentary directed by garden expert Roy Lancaster showed what an astonishing variety of winter-flowering plants still survives.

Thomas and Daniel Hanbury originally proposed not only to collect plants at La Mortola, specializing in those with economic and pharmaceutical uses, but also to conduct experiments in acclimatization, testing which species would survive in various microclimates. Most of the exotic trees in the garden date from the Hanburys' time, (an impressive *Casimiroa edulis*, for example) as well as the original collections of citrus, cacti, and other succulents. The brothers also established their famous, three hundred-meter-long pergola, with three different climbers on every pil-

lar—all manner of jasmines, passion flowers, mandevilla, thunbergias, red and yellow bignonias, as well as *Pandorea*, *Phaedranthus* (or *Distictis*), *Tecoma*, and many more. They also encouraged outlying sections of the garden to renew their natural, wild growth by preventing local shepherds from passing through. The Italian government continues to preserve with great care this rare example of unspoiled coastal scrubland or *maquis*, which covers about half the surface of La Mortola's forty acres.

The pillared gates of La Mortola admit entrance to a magic domain, the first, steep, cypress-lined steps leading down to a whole world of gardens. Many specialized plantings sit at terrace ends, with the sea as a backdrop, or cluster around the house, or inhabit the sheltered spots on the lower slopes. A map provided at the entrance ensures that the visitor will not miss any secluded corners, and lists a few of the rarest trees such as the *Araucaria cunninghamii* sown by Daniel Hanbury in June 1872. The ocher-toned tower of the restored villa can be seen from all over the garden. Its gates were brought back by Thomas from China, along with a huge temple bell in the courtyard. Just below, a stone bridge spans a restored remnant of the Roman road, the Via Aurelia. At

Despite damage resulting war and neglect, ortola still shelters -famous plant tions. Felicia ia (also "aster" or opappa") appears ny old Riviera ns (above right).

the very foot of the steep hill is an open-air tea-room, which offers welcome restoration to prepare one for the climb back up. A single visit cannot suffice to absorb the garden's riches.

Everyone will have their favorite spots: perhaps Dorothy's Australian forest area, with samples of the genera *Brachychiton*, *Acacia*, *Eucalyptus*, *Melaleuca*, and *Callistemon*. In the woodland seen from the house, huge Atlantic blue cedars and Mexican cypresses (*Cupressus guadalupensis*) shelter the old olive trees, through which Banksia roses spread, in early spring, enormous embroideries of gold. Elsewhere gentle slopes are covered with succulent plants, their infinite and surprising variations of color, shape and texture drawn from deserts all over the world. A double-ramped staircase shelters the fabulous dragon fountain from Kyoto, the beast spitting through elegant papyrus curtains. A two-tiered walk of fragrant plants, ranging from lemon-scented eucalyptus to rare lavenders, has been delightfully restored. The exotic fruit garden includes medlars, kiwis, persimmons, macadamias, and many others, lesser known. The citrus collection, with its amazing, three-pound Shattuck grapefruits, is now the center of a beautiful white garden. Perhaps one day the public will

again witness a hillside display of 115 species of brilliantly colored ice plants (*Mesembryanthemum*). Anyone wishing to take away a sketch of some favorite nook may recall that Queen Victoria did the same in 1882.

It is quite likely that every Riviera garden today contains descendants of plants which once flourished at La Mortola. Varieties of rose, agave, and aloe bear names that attest to their creation on this site. Some specialties deserve to be better known: the winter blooming roses, for example, a good selection of the nineteenth-century Nabonnands (a whole wall of 'Noelle Nabonnand'). As restoration proceeds, more and more areas are developed in the original spirit. "Long life and happiness"—so reads the ideogram over the entrance, given to Sir Thomas by the Chinese ambassador to England. One can only hope that it will protect the garden as it evolves today.

Bright yellows appear in the form of the rare Bignonia unguiscati draped over a fountain (above left), or in the ordinary double-flowered buttercup (center).

VILLA THURET

The Hanbury brothers early on exchanged plants with another collector, botanist Gustave Thuret, who in 1855 had chosen a site on Cap d'Antibes. Georges Sand visited the Villa Thuret in 1868 and described it in her correspondence as "an Eden which seems to swim in the bosom of immensity." On some seven acres, the garden and experimental station have managed to enrich immeasurably the botanical potential of the region. Linked to the national agricultural research network as of 1927, it continues to be in the vanguard, creating disease-resistant cypress varieties, for example. Two hundred new species are introduced yearly, and a new area of the garden is developed every three or four years.

The Villa Thuret is a working research garden with some three thousand species laid out for easy recognition of plant families. Aesthetic concerns are secondary here, as they once were for the Hanbury brothers. The site was chosen for its special growing conditions and provides an excellent example of the extreme variety of microclimates and soil types that can be found on the French Riviera. In this particular spot, there is 90% humidity in summer. On the north-facing slope, the temperature may regularly go down to -4° centigrade every year. Although the soil has a high degree of alkalinity, it is basic, volcanic soil, not calcareous. Many plants that will not grow on limestone thrive here. At the same time, Thuret's heavy clay maintains moisture.

All of this allows for extensive experimentation in plant adaptation. Nothing is watered or sheltered in winter—natural acclimatization is the aim. Similarly, treatments against disease and insects are kept to an absolute minimum. This, too, affects the garden's aesthetic appeal, since individual plants which are not tough enough to pass the test are left in place until their demise, as part of the experiment. The Villa Thuret nonetheless possesses some wonderful and very beautiful specimens, not least its eucalyptus and its twenty-five varieties of palms. It also has a particularly good collection of winter-flowering plants.

The Thuret Botanical Gardens contain a world of wonders even for the non-specialist: a vast variety of eucalyptus (above center) and palms (below center).

LES CÈDRES

Another legendary collector's garden owed its fame initially to King Leopold II of the Belgians, as of the 1890s. The king bought up great tracts of land on the promontory of Saint-Jean-Cap-Ferrat, growing outdoors on its sheltered slopes plants which he could only maintain under glass in his gardens at Laeken. At Saint-Jean, he cultivated even rarer flowers—such as a young Frenchwoman, sixteen-year-old Blanche Delacroix, whose secluded candy-pink domain, linked to his own by a bridge of greenery, has recently come up for sale. Another property originally purchased for the king, the Villa Mauresque, became famous as of 1928 as the home of Somerset Maugham. It is here that the writer claimed to have cultivated the first avocados on the Riviera after smuggling in the seeds in a golf bag. This was an illusion, however—Thomas Hanbury had already grown them.

In 1900, Leopold acquired the Villa Pollonais next door to his botanical gardens, a Romantic nineteenth-century domain which had opened its doors to Queen Victoria, a Bonaparte prince, and Ulysses S. Grant. In the early years of the century, this property was embellished with an Italian parterre by no less an architect than Harold Peto, whose creations at other grand villas at Saint-Jean were highlights of the period.

The domain's design elements are now largely overshadowed by its greater vocation as the most prestigious private botanical garden in the world. Rechristening it "Les Cèdres," the Marnier-Lapostolle family began collecting here in the mid-twenties. Their efforts have spread over some thirty-five acres. The gardens at Les Cèdres are laid out like a library, book by book, each one defined by a different biotype, or set of growing conditions. Some collections, like the hardy succulents, stand profiled against the dramatic sea view. Others are arranged in islands, where the taller trees and shrubs (often avocados) are carefully pruned

At Les Cèdres, immense outdoor collections g each rare specimen the exact combinati soil, sunlight, and shade it needs to thr (facing page).

The remnants of the ear Italianate design at Les Cèdres include copy of Michelange Moses, viewed here the cycad collection (following pages).

Thick stands of Phyllostachys bambusoides *(above) lead to secret corners, while the succulents cover a vast, open hillside. Novelist Kay Boyle described these plants as "thick and white as the bellies of serpents, with great horny tusks." (below).*

to let sun fall on the foliage of the lower layers. This not only provides just the right exposure, but also beautiful effects of sunlight and shadow. The great majority of plants reside in some twenty-three glasshouses, discreetly off to one side of the house and its outdoor promenades. The entire property, tended by twenty gardeners, contains more than 12,000 different species, including many large and rare trees.

A long driveway circles up toward the house, past woodland mixing common Mediterranean plants (Judas trees, cherries, and a *maquis* full of bulbs and wildflowers) with the whole spectrum of palms and other rarities. Many species are encouraged to resow themselves naturally on both sides of the drive, including the only jasmine native to Europe, echiums, and solanums now gone wild. Gaps in the foliage allow dramatic glimpses of the port of Villefranche. The bust of a Roman emperor peeks out of a shady copse. Harold Peto's now useless staircase, lined with canals on either side, leads up toward his Italianate parterre with its cypresses, parasol pines, and magnificent *Araucaria*. Far more dramatic today, however, is the large, mirror-like pond at the top of the drive, whose smooth water displays the

broad saucers of Victorias (*regia* and *cruziana*), and many rare varieties of water lilies. From here the walk of Atlas cedars (planted by the Marnier-Lapostolles) leads toward the house, lined on either side by raised beds of tiny rockery specimens. Set in limestone, but mulched with chips of red porphyry from the nearby Estérel mountains, they display an amazing range of fine foliage and floral detail: delospermas, dwarf irises, lampranthus, sedums, oxalis, mesembryanthemums and small agaves among the hundreds presented.

A formal courtyard lies in front of the house under the fierce stare of a pair of eagles on the façade. A freestanding statue of Minerva wears an imposing warrior's helmet, belied by her bemused look and the olive branch in her hand. Bright bedding plants surround her, as do majestic olive trees hung with Spanish moss and other members of the curious *Tillandsia* family. The entrance circle seems haunted by the enthusiasm of successive generations who have all made distinct contributions to this illustrious garden.

Leading away from the monumental southern porch of the house, the cycas walk shows off haunting gray and green samples of this family which existed at the time of the dinosaurs, the oldest one

The stars
...s Cèdres's amazing
...r garden are the
...er-like Victorias, at
best in autumn
...e).

here more than one hundred years old, but less than two meters tall. Arranged behind low clipped hedges (of *Lonicera nitida*), they are elegantly blended with fuchsias in the dappled shade from huge pine canopies. Here as in every part of the garden, specimens from all five continents which require similar growing conditions are grouped side by side—South Africa thus sitting comfortably between Australia and Chile. But at the same time, each space is arranged with harmonious proportions. Each of the early designers helped impose an order which the collectors have carefully adapted to their own needs. Thus the cycas walk is partially enclosed by two high pergola walls, the columns to the right still visible behind a curtain of *Jasminum polyanthum*, but those to the left completely submerged in red trumpet-flowered *Thunbergia coccinea*. Steps at the pergola's far end lead down to an Italianate perspective, a green curtain framing a copy of Michelangelo's *Moses*.

From here, curving paths, gravel-lined and stone-edged, lead into the labyrinth of rare shrub and tree collections. One may come upon the curious flame tree (with brilliant red flowers in summer but no foliage), or a rare, square-stemmed bamboo. Elsewhere a high curtain

of silvery bamboo stalks rises from a quite simple but beautiful underplanting of aspidistra. Among the roots of other trees can be found such treasures as the delicate, violet-flowered *Iris japonica*, more like a rare orchid than a simple iris. Eventually, one emerges from this carefully controlled jungle into another rockery, around extensive citrus groves, circling back under the house's long, eastern façade to the swimming pool. No other Riviera pool is quite like this one, set behind a curving stone balustrade opposite a splendid, panoramic view of the old town and the Pointe de l'Hospice to the right, Villefranche again to the left. Two stuccoed pavilions on either side add their gold balls and Egyptian red vaults to the turquoise of the pool itself to complete the Côte d'Azur décor. But by far the greatest theatrical effect of this site comes from the vast bank of succulents, in every imaginable shape and color, rising between the pool and the house above. Through it, paths meander, contained by low hedges of *Lampranthus haworthii*, looking like upright-growing versions of the semi-succulent plant commonly called "witch's teeth," but covered with bright yellow flowers. Rising from the heart of this massive display are the nineteenth-century date palms

Les Cèdres possesses the world's largest collection of the Bromeliad family, including this Spanish moss or Old Man's Beard (Tillandsia usneoides) swinging from an olive tree (below).

planted by the Pollonais family, the first cosmopolitan owners of this once-rustic farm.

But rich as the outdoor garden proves to be, it shrinks in comparison with the plants arranged, with surprising decorative impact, in the twenty-two glasshouses. Some also shelter tropical birds, ponds, or present their treasures among draped curtains of multicolored bougainvilleas. The most famous collections are the succulents, the epiphytic plants (particularly the bromeliads) and the huge variety of trees. Head gardener René Hebding is the high priest of these mysteries. Roderick Cameron, owner and designer of another fabulous garden nearby, commented after several visits in the company of the learned curator: "Each time I come away feeling I have travelled thousands of miles." The gardens are indeed so vast that it is hard to encompass them all at once. While maintaining a solid reputation in the world of botanists, Les Cèdres still upholds the lavish spirit of the old Riviera with a panache all its own.

VILLA ILE DE FRANCE

King Leopold was not quick enough to obtain the nearby seventeen acres at the entrance to the peninsula of Saint-Jean-Cap-Ferrat, which Baroness Béatrice Ephrussi de Rothschild transformed just before World War I. Clearly visible from Les Cèdres, as well as from Beaulieu and Villefranche on either side, the domain rides the sea like an ocean liner—or so thought the baroness, for she named the property after the huge transatlantic ship, the *Ile de France*. At one point, thirty-five gardeners are said to have worked energetically here, dressed as sailors with red-pomponned berets. The gardens were laid out like an invitation to travel: the Spanish next to the Florentine, leading into the Japanese and so on. Only the east slope was left unfinished because, in spite of the colossal fortune available, funds ran out. It has remained as the Provençal Garden, full of rosemaries, terebinths, box, pines, and other plants familiar from the local wild hillsides, known as *garrigue*.

This project was, from the start, gardening as spectacle on a grand scale. Here, more than in any other site, the earthworks were legendary: having chosen the windiest spot in the area, the baroness was determined not to be limited by "the stupid laws of nature and common sense." The hilltop was flattened to make an esplanade some three hundred meters long and forty wide. The villa's construction was begun in 1910, the building intended to house, as it still does today, the baroness's fabulous collections of art and furniture. Numerous architects tried their hand at this imitation of a Venetian *palazzino*, some constructing large-as-life models of the façade in wood and canvas. Trains full of antiques and dismantled Italian palaces, or carved woodwork from the Hotel Crillon in Paris, were unloaded at the station in Villefranche, where Madame de Rothschild, dressed in her beloved pink, chose what she wanted—marble columns from Verona for the house patio, for example. Completed in 1912, her domain was abandoned in 1915 when she got divorced and moved to Monaco, leaving funds for the upkeep of her collections.

Today the much-visited villa and its gardens belong to the French Institute. Active restoration of the garden has been taking place since 1987. The Spanish Garden, just below the house to the east and first in the sequence of visits, was cleared of the rubble caused by the patio above caving in. Two amphorae from Grenada were preserved and provide Spanish atmosphere. Above all, this emanates from intimate strips of quiet water enclosed in a cloister-like square of high walls and surrounded by formal arrangements of pomegranates (called Grenada trees in French), seconded by tree-sized daturas. The triple colonnade which separates this garden from the next supports lush pergola plantings, including a rare climber which the gardener, Mr. Vitale, calls *Bossiaea yervamora*. Once a net extended from the patio above these arches to keep in the white ibis which inhabited this garden.

Beyond the Spanish Garden lies Italy—though once again, the naming is somewhat fanciful. Banks of flowers surround an imposing baroque staircase leading up to the house level; at the top, the staircase is flanked by cypress arches and espaliered wisteria which thus provide the backdrop for the scene below. Here each season has its glories: mimosas are followed by mounds of rhaphiolepis. In summer, agapanthus beds,

The Villa Ile de France and its garden are a mosaic of cultures, fragments and travel memories. Kay Boyle's image suits this place well: "Green stalks of flowering marble and the false deep sea. . . ." Béatrice de Rothschild's loving pastiche suited the taste of her times (center and facing page).

*In front
of the Villa Ile de
France, undulating
hedges separate
the formal French
garden from the theme
gardens (Spanish,
Florentine, Japanese,
etc.) facing Villefranche
to the west (above).
Hedging and elaborate
bedding were once
maintained by a
regiment of gardeners
wearing sailor hats.*

bougainvillea, and a pair of *Acacia farnesiana* flower together. Rare specimens stand among unpretentious clumps of oleander. The grotto and pool lying between the flight of steps are shaded by the discreet climber *Holboellia latifolia*, whose scent is so powerful and pervasive in the spring. Near a much smaller, hidden baroque fountain further downhill stands a curious *Nolina*, a palm-like tree with bark like a cork oak's. The only Florentine feature here is a long cypress lane which has momentarily lost its focal point.

Then comes the Lapidary Garden, full of stone fragments not used in the house, including an elegant Roman door frame. This part is shaded by redbuds and a camphor tree, outlined (as often elsewhere) with bands of upright sedums, *Felicia filifolium* (often called "aster" by Riviera gardeners), impatiens and bergenia.

The Japanese Garden is named for its oriental-looking, miniature stone and ceramic houses ensconced in densely shaded banks of bamboo; shiny, round-leaved *Ligularia tussilaginea*; and acanthus. Its dark enclosure contrasts strikingly with the cactus spikes and mounds amid rock piles in the Exotic Garden next door. Beyond that, oval beds of Meilland roses, laid out on several levels and topped by a series of columns to support recently planted climbers, curve round the southeastern tip of the promontory.

The sinuous paths which connect different levels are often accompanied by curious, rustic balustrades of cement, fashioned to look like twisting branches, part of the garden's original, theatrical décor. One such ramp now leads back toward the villa, upward through a wooded area, through a section once designated "English" but not yet restored. Here, amidst tall Aleppo pines, stands the domain's crowning glory, the Temple to Love, which faces the Venetian house façade some three hundred meters distant. The temple is situated at the garden's original ground level; looking down toward the house, one is amazed at the amount of earth originally removed—down to bedrock. Soil to a depth of just two meters was then put back for planting, with the result that the oldest cypresses now have roots that spread horizontally all over the garden.

The canal linking hill and house, edged with colorful annuals and spreading into a round basin which reflects the façade, provides the garden's most photographed axis. In the baroness's time, it was lined with bright turquoise tiles. Today it shelters two tortoises abandoned there by visitors. The symmetrical plantings around urns on pedestals and twin cloverleaf basins on either side have been deemed "French" because of their formal arrangement, although their plantings also involve wisterias trained as standards, soaring and squat palm trees, and giant Formosa agaves stretching, like giant, lopsided pineapples, toward the winter sun.

Thus concludes the grand tour, greatly appreciated by an ever-broadening audience. The Villa Ile de France offers one of the few grand old gardens open to the public—as was its creator's intention. Perhaps one of the greatest attractions here for apprentice gardeners is the remarkable wealth of adaptable

The ...ern side of the Villa ...le France ...looks the wild, ...vençal garden ...rd Beaulieu.

groundcovers displayed among the rare specimens—a discreet feature in gardens which remain absolutely spectacular, not least because of the many carefully framed viewpoints giving on to the harbors on both sides.

This property is sometimes criticized for having too much of a public park atmosphere and style, but one could argue that this was the dominating spirit of the place from its very beginnings. With some differences: once a host of gardeners set out some 45,000 annual bedding plants whereas today three struggle with 12,000. These gardens do present, however, a sometimes strange mix of the rare and the banal, the exotic and the commonplace. It should be remembered, in their favor, that they were created at a time when leaders in the "higher" arts were praising pastiche as the very fount of modern creativity, and they— just like Béatrice de Rothschild—heaped scorn on both nature and common sense! Such mixtures of period and genre, already frequent enough in Riviera gardens before her efforts, are precisely what made the whole region avant-garde for its time. They spring from a conception of art which indeed celebrates chance encounter, or (in the memorable phrase of philosopher Susan Sontag) "art that is produced not by pregnancy and childbirth but by a blind date." Whether this approach to time (near-instantaneous creation) and chance (seemingly random arrangements) can be accepted as part of the art of gardening, where slow ripening usually prevails, is another question; the Villa Rothschild clearly echoes the fashions of its time. The blind date, after all, implies a party, a

fête—much the mood of the avant-garde in the Belle Epoque. And much the best spirit in which to enjoy these gardens today.

LA GAROUPE

Saint-Jean-Cap-Ferrat was not the only barren headland to shelter the glow and festivities of cosmopolitan glamour. Cap d'Antibes was at least equally distinguished. Grand Duke Nicolas of Russia spent time here, as did the duke and duchess of Windsor and Umberto of Italy, and writers such as Jules Verne and Anatole France. Winston Churchill painted splendid sea views from the Villa Horizon, built for American actress Maxine Elliott. Guy de Maupassant already described the whole spur as "a long rocky point, a marvellous garden thrown between two oceans where the most beautiful flowers of Europe are grown. . . ."

In 1922, composer Cole Porter had the eccentric idea of spending the summer on Cap d'Antibes. He rented a villa called the Château de la Garoupe, which, like all other cosmopolitan Riviera villas at that time, was abandoned by its owners in the summer. A mad band of bohemian Americans followed him to Cap d'Antibes that year, Scott and Zelda Fitzgerald being the most famous if not the most popular. The nearby Hôtel du Cap was kept open over the summer to accommodate them. Porter never returned, but the following year his role as host fell to another legendary couple, Gerald and Sara Murphy. They gradually restored an old domain to create their own Villa America, with one of

The current owner of La Garoupe, Anthony Norman, conceived this stunning parterre of santolina, lavender, and rosemary (following pages).

the coast's very first sun roofs, and launched the summer season which has persisted ever since.

The Murphys' Riviera adventures have been vividly described in Calvin Tomkin's chronicle, *Living Well is the Best Revenge*. Their "art of living" was highly commended by friends such as Picasso, Stravinsky, Dos Passos, Hemingway, Gertrude Stein and Alice B. Toklas, and Archibald MacLeish. It centered on their garden. Gerald, after all, had begun life as a landscape designer before becoming a painter. They chose a property belonging to a French army officer long stationed in the Near East, who had planted "date palms, Arabian maples with pure-white leaves, pepper trees, olives, ever-bearing

At La Garoupe, the garden's main axis runs through the vast, formal parterre, plunging down to the rocky coastline below. The proportions of this grand design have been perfectly balanced to frame the view.

Meanwhile, the Hôtel du Cap, which had housed the Murphys and their friends while work was completed on the Villa America, later drew all the stars of Hollywood and has since been pursuing its own legends as one of the greatest of the Riviera "palaces." The imposing villa next door, Eden Roc, a Belle Epoque property redesigned in the 1930s, has now become a twenty-two–acre arboretum belonging to the city of Antibes.

Another destiny awaited the Château de la Garoupe, which Cole Porter rented in that first, fateful summer of 1922. Indeed, it had already achieved celebrity well before his arrival and today, still evolving, it remains the pride of Cap d'Antibes. There is nothing of the blind date here, but three generations

lemon trees, black and white figs—all of which had prospered and proliferated. Heliotrope and mimosa ran wild through the garden, which flowed down from the house in a series of levels, intersected by gravel paths. There was hardly a flower that would not grow there, for it was on the side of a hill that was protected from the mistral. At night, the whole place throbbed with nightingales." An idyllic party given on their terraces is described in Fitzgerald's *Tender is the Night*, a novel dedicated to "Gerald and Sara, many fêtes." He depicts the Murphys in their garden as a special oasis of civilization, a kind of modern-day Thélème which made better all who were privileged to share it. Picasso also admired the Murphys' hospitality, saying of Sara that she was "très festin."

of slow ripening in the hands of talented and knowledgeable gardeners.

The Château de la Garoupe was built by Lady Aberconway in 1905-1907 as the winter counterpart to her summer property at Bodnant, in North Wales. Among fifty-five acres of rocky, dry hillside, smothered in thyme, rockroses, myrtle, and medicago, twelve acres of garden sprang to life. Lady Aberconway's daughter became a regular summer resident in the 1920s, restoring a flower farm which at that time existed on the property near the beach. She passed her love of gardening along to her son, Anthony Norman, the present and third-generation owner. Since his grandmother's death in 1934, there have been important changes, in particular a shift toward spring and summer flowering which nonetheless respects the original design.

The imposing house, Italianate in style, dominates the property from its hilltop in the center of the garden. Its main façade faces south. A strong central axis leads right through the house from the north slope, then plunges south down a formal staircase toward the tip of the rocky beach below. This descent to the sea, with its 130 shallow, white marble-faced steps, is surrounded by cypress towers, bands of oleanders, yucca swords and stipa, aloes, bupleurum balls, yellow-daisied medicago, silver convolvulus, blue lithospermum, purple *Carpobrotus edulis*, and splashes of bright pelargoniums. It must count among the most photographed views of any French Riviera garden.

points spread wedges of lavender (the *pinnata* variety), rosemary, gray and green santolinas. The effect is of great formality and strong lines, but there is also movement in the design, which was inspired by the Piazza del Populo in Rome. It looks as striking from either end, on a level, as it does from above. Though sections of it are often in flower (even the santolinas are allowed to bloom), the colors remain soft and subdued and they set off rather than compete with the sea view beyond. The surrounding lawn has stands of pines and gold-leaved robinias. All these billowing shapes and shades of green contrast beautifully with the dark cypress pillars.

The panorama from the broad terrace which runs along the south façade of the

Paths
through La Garoupe's
southern gardens are
lined with jewel-like
purple iris and deep
pink cyclamen (center).

The sea is an ever-present partner at La Garoupe. Cypress pillars are carefully spaced to frame it from the house, setting off the frequent passage of distant sails. The descent's powerful axis is balanced by a strong horizontal pull: a pair of summer houses (designed by Felix Kelly in *trompe l'oeil* fretwork) rises gracefully among the trees at each end of a broad terrace cutting across the hillside below the house. The harmonious proportions of this design anchor the garden to the southern hillside and enhance the famous double parterre which lies at the heart of the composition.

Here Anthony Norman imagined the garden's most original and impressive feature: a geometric pattern around two Venetian vases, encircled with box cones. From these focal

house is vast, encompassing a whole series of gardens east and west as well as the parterre in front, the steps and the sea below. To the west, a giant Aleppo pine stands guard over the distant prospect. Colorful borders close to the house lead toward box-edged citrus balls against a curtain of red datura trumpets in the middle distance, above which two more cypress pillars frame carefully layered greenery, ending with tall oaks at the back. Within this well-composed scene, however, the scale changes: on close inspection, a whole series of small, secret gardens is revealed, a labyrinth of masterfully enclosed spaces joined by a few stone steps leading up or down into yet other, unexpected corners.

First is the *jardin de curé* with its formal arrangement of four dwarf box-edged beds

F. Scott Fitzgerald, once Cole Porter's guest at La Garoupe, admired "kaleidoscopic peonies massed in pink clouds . . . fragile mauve-stemmed roses, transparent like sugar flowers in a confectioner's window." (above and center).

around an astrolabe. Each section contains taller box towers and orange trees in Italian terracotta urns. A stone bench is hung round with silvery foliage of a weeping pear tree (*Pyrus salicifolia* 'Pendula').

The north wall supports a pergola, whose stone pillars are variously and fragrantly bedecked with star jasmine, roses, a rare passion flower *Passiflora allardii*. Ancient wisterias mount high in even older olive trees. An alcove lined with brilliant Persian tiles long served as a tea room, and is now the antechamber to a new area around the swimming pool.

Designed to look as much as possible like a lake, the latter's broad rectangle is surrounded by much brilliant bloom. Pelargoniums, fuchsias, gazanias, lantanas, and lagerstroemias mingle reds, pinks, oranges, and purples, carefully blended with whites (including arum lilies) and the blue spikes of echium. Oleanders trained as standards are one of Mr. Norman's specialties.

A few steps lead down to the white garden, the most secluded of all. Here a circle of citrus provides cooling shade around an octagonal pond, where water lilies indolently float. Hebe 'White Gem', oak-leaved hydrangeas, and 'Mme Lemoine' lilacs thrive here, around an inviting marble bench. Thus ends the series of gardens, the most intimate spaces on the property, although there is a fine attention to detail and texture throughout.

The overall design at La Garoupe harmoniously combines two common types of Riviera plan: the terraced slope, and the hilltop encircled by a series of gardens. Moving east of the house, one discovers plantings that have been left more open, less formal: a kind of sophisticated *garrigue* spreads under tall pines, including rare rockroses (*cistus*), small golden conifers next to pale purple-bloomed lavateras, and darker purple *Lavandula stoechas*, pavonias, and many creeping and mounding rock plants (euryops, creeping asters or *Felicia filifolium*, star-flowered delospermas, and much more). The sea is still a presence: from the eastern summer house, Corsica lies just below the horizon and its shadow can be seen on the water at sunrise.

Circling north, one discovers the new gold and yellow garden, created to celebrate the Normans' golden wedding anniversary. It mixes, informally, gold-leaved *Philadelphus*; spireas; honeysuckles and shrubby dogwoods set off by dark red arctotis with its gray, woolly foliage; pale purple and pink-flowering lavateras; more delosperma; hibiscus; and two standard 'Soleil d'Or' Meilland

At La [Garo]upe, a wisteria-[cover]ed pergola of five [arches] runs [along] the back wall, [with] alcoves and [niche]s, and on toward [the s]wimming pool [(followi]ng page).

roses. As a backdrop stand more golden robinias, seconded this time by 'Sunburst' snail trees (*Gleditsias*) and mimosas.

Finally, one arrives at the wild-looking north slope. It, too, has its plunging staircase, flanked at house level by the striking sentinels of male and female cycas. Below, sheets of bulbs (white narcissus in December, freesias in April) echo the winter and spring mixes of pink and white bloom as first almond trees (including the oldest one on Cap d'Antibes), then magnolias and flowering cherries give way to Judas trees, all set off by the crowns of ancient olive trees with swaths of purple-blue iris at their feet.

Mr. Norman insists that La Garoupe is not a collector's garden, in which rarity of specimens commands attention for its own sake (though he also has arboretum areas for plants which interest him). Nor is it a garden given over to flowers, which, in his view, are but the final part of the design. He is much concerned with the exact placement of trees and shrubs in the pattern, and does not hesitate to transplant even large specimens. But there is no doubt that La Garoupe is dense with bloom, and bright with color in every season. And its brilliance, sometimes almost overwhelming, should reassure those timid souls who fear red flowers in a garden. Of course, they are always modulated with white. Mr. Norman has a special gift, moreover, for using golden-foliaged plants, not only in the yellow garden but overall. At La Garoupe, they never shock or look merely sick, as they so often do elsewhere in the south.

La Garoupe has often been described as a grand garden, "sumptuous," or a "showplace." Many of its effects are spectacular and certainly the large scale of its particularly well-balanced design justifies these epithets. At the same time, however, because of its riotous and exuberant flowers, it has a homey, almost cottage feel: in the borders Anthony Norman recently planted just around the house, Banksia roses and bougainvilleas scramble up around the shutters, amidst the blue spikes of *Echium candicans*, while Meilland roses tumble over balustrades. The atmosphere is neither awesome nor imposing, but intimate and welcoming.

VILLA ROQUEBRUNE

The same might be said of another grand garden on yet another famous promontory, Cap Martin, which for decades received the empress Eugénie and her friends. Here lies a magical domain perched even more dramatically on a sea slope than La Garoupe, and like it influential through several genera-

tions: the Villa Roquebrune, created by a private English gardener of great talent, Norah Warre. The site, a stark accumulation of limestone boulders, proved daunting at first view; when her first husband took her there in 1902, Mrs. Warre is said to have burst into tears, saying "But I wanted to make a garden!" She managed thereafter to cultivate this five-acre plot for seventy-five years. When blind in advanced age, she nonetheless went round to check on her beloved plants, judging by feel and smell— for Roquebrune certainly counts among the most fragrant of Riviera gardens.

Like the Normans, Mrs. Warre always welcomed visits from other Riviera gardeners, traded plants and ideas, and served as an inspiration to several generations. She was very much a collector, and her garden contains many gifts from friends—including the *Jasminum polyanthum* which Lawrence Johnston, creator of the influential English gardens at Hidcote Manor, brought back from Yunnan. The plant is used artfully as a hedge with shrubby germander (*Teucrium fruticans*) along the rim of the cliff, with the sea behind. Gifts and advice came also from other leaders in the British garden world, such as nurseryman Sir Harold Hillier, and from the directors of famous plant collections at Kew and Wisley gardens.

Once tons of earth and manure had been secured behind high terrace walls, plantations began. They succeeded so well that the olive and pine trees of early days are now lost in a soft, woodland effect. In a long article on Roquebrune by Basil Leng and Patrick M. Synge for the *Royal Horticultural Society Journal*, written during Mrs. Warre's lifetime, the authors claim they cannot begin to cope with the overwhelming list of rare species and cultivars they found. But all of their descriptions stress exuberance: hillsides of lantanas and mesembryanthemums, each color in swaths several meters across; delicate-flowered *Hebe hulkeanas* massed "with a solid abundance rarely seen in England." Underplantings included gray-leaved plants, artemisias, gazanias, chrysanthemums, *Agave americana*, which still thrive today among tall shrubs like the white-flowered broom so beloved of flower arrangers, *Genista monosperma*; or *Petrea volubilis* (the purple wreath from Mexico) or free-flowering *Buddleja madagascariensis*. The climbers were not the least enthusiastic growers and still invade a series of pergolas, or drape down the terrace walls, some of which, after all, are four meters high: akebia battles with *Holboellia latifolia* near a 'Madame Grégoire Staechelin' rose. Many varieties of jasmine

The bird-of-paradise flo Strelitzia regina, added its strange brilliance to many e gardens, where exotic color was eminently desirable The Villa Roquebru still survives on Caj Martin, facing the l blue spur of Monac in the distance.

and bignonia still proliferate, and a single plant of *Solandra hartwegii* suffices to smother the balustrade behind the house with its huge, golden trumpet flowers.

Today, as in Mrs. Warre's time, lines of terracing are lost in a profusion of plants, so that it is almost impossible to find any long perspective or general overview. Yet on this hillside laced with curving paths, where it is very easy to get lost, each advance means new discovery. Many finds suddenly emerge profiled against the nearby sea.

Here too, the Mediterranean is framed by exotic trees now majestically old and frequently rare: a twelve-meter-tall *Grevillea robusta*, an evergreen maple (*Acer longifolia*), a venerable jacaranda, a semi-evergreen Cape chestnut (*Calodendrum capense*) with flowers like delicate, rosy orchids, and two enormous, spreading, blue Portuguese cypresses.

Roquebrune was conceived above all for dazzling winter and spring bloom, for Mrs. Warre faithfully returned to England every summer throughout her long career. In March and April, bulbs and flowers make a stunning tapestry. There is brilliance year-round, however. Blue towers of echiums, scarlet *Russelias* threading among the aloes, orange and blue darts of *Strelitzias*, set off the exotic forms of cycas and cacti, seconded by carissas, dombeyas, red and yellow abutilons, masses of purple polygalas, rare pittosporums and hebes, and similar hordes of exotic flowers impossible to grow in any other climate. Many plants happily self-sow here: among them are deep blue convolvulus and paler cynoglossum. Nor does all this wealth grow in chaotic confusion: each corner has its own design and character. Thus echiums and *Polygala myrtifolia* make a striking, early spring, blue and purple composition rising above a carpet of deep pink dimorphotheca. And then there is the magnificent collection of more than twenty rambling roses: *Rosa gigantea* and *R.* 'La Follette', *R.* 'Lorraine Lee', *R.* 'Ramona', *R. cooperii*, *R. laevigata*, *R.* 'Gloire de Dijon', and *R. henryi*, among them.

After a period of neglect, the Villa Roquebrune and its hillside have been restored and divided into a co-property, with an obligation on all the joint owners to maintain the gardens. There have been some failures: the collection of rare mimosas has in part declined due to excessive watering by inexperienced gardeners. And some modern adaptations have been necessary: broad expanses of lawn, a swimming pool and tennis court have replaced some parts of the original rockery. One lovely lower corner, somewhat formal in its design of crisscrossing pergolas, awaits a restoration which could make it one of the finest parts of the garden.

Those who work to rehabilitate Roquebrune keep discovering species and varieties which experts have trouble identifying. This garden has not yet unveiled all its hidden treasures. Its spirit is still exuberant, dense, and brilliant. Mrs. Warre's ghost may soon feel at home here once again.

LE CLOS DU PEYRONNET

Nearby, the city of Menton, in particular the sheltered Garavan Bay, witnessed a whole flowering of fine gardens in the early twentieth century. The only one to thrive without interruption is the Clos du Peyronnet. Three generations of the Waterfield family created this garden on a terraced hillside overlooking the sea, one of the smallest perhaps (encompassing only one acre) but certainly one of the most influential.

In 1915, Derrick and Barbara Waterfield purchased the property with its nineteenth-century Italianate house and terraces punctuated by olive trees and cypresses. Their son Humphrey, a painter and landscaper well known in England, laid out the lines of the present garden in the 1950s. After his death, his nephew William took on the garden. Today, the latter's jovial, bearded face is commonly seen at plant fairs and garden shows in the area, where, accompanied by his ever-present Jack Russell terriers, he exhibits, trades, and usually gives away rare specimens. William Waterfield specializes in bulbs, but has maintained and extended every aspect of his legacy with all the care which a single pair of hands and undiminished passion for the task can provide.

The driveway forms a circle in front of the colonnaded house façade, where the force of a Chinese wisteria has broken one of the pillars in most romantic fashion. Within the circle and along the border of the drive are

The gardens [at Ro]quebrune contain [many] varieties of [mimo]sa (Acacia) and [acac]ias, like this [lar]ge-flowered [aca]cia siamensis, first [impo]rted by Lawrence [John]ston in 1934 [followi]ng page).

Norah Warre, creator of the fabulous gardens at Villa Roquebrune, enjoyed the arabesque of their paths and terraces for some seventy-five years (center).

At the Clos du Peyronnet, the nineteenth-century villa's entrance is nearly smothered in wisteria *(above).*

Orange Chasmanthi floribundi *and purple echium strike a bold contrast in April (below).*

already a number of rare species of *Oreopanax* and *Acacia*, a big *Nolina*, jacaranda, and a catalpa, under two huge *Washingtonia* palms. A climbing *Beaumontia* cascades on one corner of the house.

East of the villa, through a shrub grove, extend two broad terraces, the heart of the garden. Here are twin rectangular pools, one about forty centimeters higher than the other. The line between them has been put to best advantage by a plantation of opalescent *Zephyranthes candida*, doubled by its own reflection. A stone-pillared pergola reaches along the back wall of the patio, underlined by white arum or calla lilies at its foot. It shades welcoming benches and a table from summer heat, its columns entwined with jasmine, star jasmine, and blue-trumpeted thunbergias. A single column supports a 'Black Dragon' wisteria, an orange-flowered *Tropaeolum* and a pale pink rose, all flowering together in early May.

Unusual urns and pots (including two enormous jars in the Medici style) stand at the turn of a path, or the end of a perspective against the high eastern wall, whose warm ocher tones are curtained in greenery. The hillside rises sharply to the north, shrubbery with many rare varieties encloses this

space east and west, only the sea view lies open to the south.

The largest part of the Clos du Peyronnet gardens lies on the upper slope, where narrow terraces are dominated by the silvery peak of the mountain crest above Menton. From the uppermost reaches, a series of increasingly large ponds descends from level to level to the twin rectangular pools by the house, which then give onto the broad, blue expanse of the sea below—a watery, staircase effect which is one of Humphrey's most celebrated achievements.

William Waterfield, very much the plantsman ever in need of more space, has further enriched the composition he inherited. Today, a dramatic pattern of tiered, small pots set below a Judas tree canopy, two ancient olive trees, and the brilliant yellow flowers of *Senecio petasites* command all the eye's attention in this section of the garden, at least in early spring. The scene dazzles from below—but close examination of the pots is necessary to appreciate the beauty and rarity of their carefully cultivated contents. Some plants are displayed on sixteen small, square tables for easier inspection of their delicate shapes and nuances of color.

Closer to the house, a more formal flight of broad, stone steps provides a

William Waterfield strolls, Adam in Eden, through his wild ga (facing page).

strong, vertical axis up the hillside, culminating in a plaque commemorating the garden's founders. Here each level has its own large and highly decorative terracotta urns, each brimming over with succulents of various color and habit. William Waterfield has carefully matched their shapes and colors to those of their containers.

As is often the case, the vertical sweep provides drama, but mystery resides in the secluded ends of the horizontal terraces. Behind and above the house, more steps lead to a triple stone arch, west of which stretches an orchard mingling avocados, guavas, citrus, loquats, a vine whose grapes have a curious raspberry flavor, collections of solanums, and heat-loving hibiscus. To the east extends a whole series of much-photographed cypress arches, tree pairs with their tops joined above the path—"cut neat and narrow but slightly wayward in shape so that they resemble nothing so much as distorted green smoke rings," says historian Charles Quest-Ritson, who considers the Peyronnet the best modern garden in the south of France.

Plants have been grown or kept for many reasons here—one somewhat scraggly elder serves to ward off witches, according to local lore. Humble plants are not despised; hollyhocks are allowed to sow where they will.

The density of plants concentrated in this garden is quite simply incredible. All sizes, colors, shapes, smells, and no doubt tastes are represented. Some of the rarer items include the climbing *Beaumontia* cascading on one corner of the house, or the comparatively new collection of nerines; but there are also more familiar presences: tender sages and daturas, grevilleas, and melaleucas.

The entire list would be overwhelming. Each generation of Waterfields participated in the small but active circle of garden enthusiasts who shared so generously, and there are plants here from all the other legend-making properties. And even two terracotta urns made for Lawrence Johnston, marked with his initials, on the house terrace.

GARDENS OF MENTON

The city of Menton has been singularly blessed in its garden heritage. Its particularly privileged climate has drawn some of the

most important garden designers of the century, and, although many of their creations are now in a pitiful state, awaiting problematic restoration, at least they have not been razed and replaced by apartment buildings.

The two most influential gardens of Menton were created by two giants among contemporary gardeners, one English and one French: Lawrence Johnston at the Serre de la Madone, and Ferdinand Bac at Les Colombières.

Johnston first came, like so many others, for health reasons: his mother sojourned in a sanatorium in Gorbio and he himself had been gassed during World War I. He suspected that the plant treasures he brought back from exotic lands would flourish in Menton's gentle climate and decided to create his own garden to house them. He chose a self-contained site, with no sea view, a terraced hillside in the Gorbio valley called the Serre de la Madone. He wintered there for many years, spending summers at his famous property, Hidcote Manor, now one of England's most visited gardens. In later years he lived in Menton full-time until his death in 1958.

The house sits at the top of the garden, and below it, steps and basins, elaborated by fountains and sculpture, create a strong central axis. Two open, rectangular pools lie at the heart of the garden on the same level, where an elegant *orangerie* faces an equally distinguished eighteenth-century statue—one of the garden's Madonnas, sometimes known as Mrs. Johnston.

The terraces on either side of the vertical descent each have their own character, but there is always a focal point of some kind at the end of the perspective. Another, less obvious itinerary winds from the entrance up the hillside, around the garden's outer reaches; but in both cases one moves between open vistas and closed spaces, from surprise to surprise. About half of the fifteen-acre property is thus landscaped, and the transition into surrounding wilderness is carefully orchestrated.

Inevitably, the creator of Hidcote cared as much about plants, for both color and texture, as design—though the latter aspect of the garden has survived better than the former. He excelled in layered masses of shrubs, bulbs, and flowers—whole banks and slopes

Two legendary features of the Clos du Peyronnet: the column broken by the force of an enormous wisteria (preceding pages); and the water staircase created by Humphrey Waterfield, a succession of pools descending toward the sea (center).

of plantings such as starry pink *Amaryllis belladonna* rising from carpets of blue plumbago. From his plant forays to the Far East he brought back the rare mahonias, *M. siamensis* and *M. lomariifolia*, which have now self-sown throughout the garden. He collected double-flowered tree peonies, and wisterias from Japan. There were flowers in all seasons, many extremely rare but always grouped for the pleasure of the eye.

Ferdinand Bac, by contrast, was not at all a horticulturist, nor even a collector, but the defender of native plants—one might even say a worshiper. The olive and the cypress reigned in his gardens, though in one case, at Les Colombières, a bridge was built especially to honor an ancient carob tree. From his travels he brought back not plants but all manner of allusions, be it in garden styles (Andalusian, Tuscan), garden architecture and décor (*fabriques* with echoes of Palladio) or even literary inscriptions (from Homer). His subtle color sense created symphonies of green and gray that stood in contrast to the ocher tones of local architecture—although his buildings' famous Venetian red wash was inspired by Carpaccio rather than local Menton tradition. This particular color range and his interest in landscape geometries are suggestive of Cézanne, who of course took his inspiration from western Provence. Bac's gardens were quite the opposite of Johnston's also in that they were not at all self-contained but "borrowed" the surrounding landscape most dramatically— Les Colombières gives onto snowy Alpine peaks in one direction, onto Garavan Bay and the old town of Menton in another, each vista carefully framed to best effect. This great love of majestic panoramas was part of a desire to enhance the natural site, though here, too, as with Johnston, the transition from garden into landscape was gradual.

Like Johnston, Bac treated house and garden as a single unit (something landscape architects began to do regularly on the Riviera in the 1920s). Johnston's inspiration was both British and worldwide, Bac's was rather pan-Mediterranean. Johnston conceived a sequence of enclosed garden rooms, Bac imagined Les Colombières like a cathedral, with so many vast chapels. This was his last

garden; invited by the owners to begin work in 1919, he lived at Les Colombières from 1926 until his death in 1952. Their three tombs were reverently placed together in one part of the garden. Bac's mood was indeed almost mystic, infinite rather than intimate, and Les Colombières is populated by gods and goddesses, rather than rare plants. But perhaps these are merely different forms of veneration?

Among Menton's other important vestiges is the Villa Maria Serena, created by Charles Garnier for Ferdinand de Lesseps (designer of the Suez Canal). It now hosts official receptions among its extensive collections of exotica. Another property overlooking Garavan Bay is the fabulous Fontana Rosa, the fanciful domain of Spanish novelist Blasco Ibañez, containing many unusual fragments of ceramic-tiled garden architecture and statues of the author's heroes. In western Menton, the park surrounding the art museum at the Palais Carnolès displays fifty varieties of citrus in a pleasant promenade.

The Parc du Pian on the hillside above the town is laid out on terraces bearing thousand-year-old olive trees. Next door lies one of Menton's most interesting domains: the Belle Epoque villa of Val Rahmeh. English collector Miss Campbell created here in the 1950s a colorfully exotic botanical garden on two acres of hillside. The National Museum of Natural History now maintains it as a southern counterpart to the Jardins des Plantes in Paris, specializing in exotic fruit varieties and in ethnobotany (the cultural uses of plants, particularly as relating to the *Solanaceae* family which includes an imposing range from tomatoes to tobacco).

Many English names in the Old Cemetery bear witness to the city's role as a not-so-successful shelter for consumptives. This spot was much admired by Maupassant who exclaimed: "What a place this would be to live in, this garden where the dead sleep. Roses, roses, roses everywhere . . . their violent perfume stifles, makes heads and legs unsteady." One visitor who came often to Menton for her health was Katherine Mansfield. She loved the gardens at her rented villa, Isola Bella, as she had never loved any place but her home, and praised warmly, in her letters to her husband, John Middleton

Harold Nicolson, Vita Sackville-West's husband, admired Johnston's "calculated alternance of suspense and surprise." Here a double pool lies open to the sky amidst more secret garden rooms (following pages).

Murray, "the smell of the full summer sea and the bay tree in the gardens and the smell of lemons." This property, too, still exists and awaits restoration.

These are but a few of Menton's celebrated domains, which both enrich and impoverish the municipality today. Open to the public only under special circumstances at the moment, many may well become accessible in the near future.

HILLTOP GARDENS AT HYERES

The period between the two world wars produced an incredible range of garden experimentation, both in design and horticulture—and sometimes in combinations of both. These properties were not only brilliant in their bloom, but also by their reputations and that of their visitors. Edith Wharton's elaborate Castel Sainte-Claire overlooking the old town of Hyères competed with the nearby Villa Noailles, whose owners counted among the most avant-garde art patrons of the period. Poet Paul Valéry visited both, and Man Ray shot his *Mystères du château de Dé* at the Noailles property. Marie-Laure de Noailles long presided here over a brilliantly talented court of artists, writers, sculptors, and composers in an opulent, bohemian, sometimes scandalous manner, which had all the panache and poetry of her time.

Here Robert Mallet-Stevens created an impressively avant-garde villa in the 1920s with high, ocher-toned walls, large square windows and a whole series of inner courtyards. At the east end, in a triangle behind high walls, Gabriel Guévrékian imagined a cubist garden which survives in its general outline today, a checkerboard pattern organized in a space much like the prow of a ship. Plants here are interchangeable, of no interest in their own right, as long as the design is maintained. This venture belongs perhaps more to the history of architecture than to that of gardening.

The Villa Noailles and Castel Sainte-Claire sit together on different flanks of the same hillside. Both look down on a sea of old-tiled roofs and a stone church tower, with a bright blue strip of sea far beyond. Between the properties lie extensive archeological digs, revealing vestiges of a community which flourished here from the fifth to eighth centuries. Curious tunnels and systems of interconnecting wells on different levels have been discovered. This

*V*al Rahmeh *in Menton is beautiful in all seasons but especially in autumn, when its tree-size datura are magnificently set off by the dusky blue of* Solanum rantonnettii *(center and below).*

*P*owder-blue Plumbago capensis a[nd] *orange lantana cascade over a wall below the Villa Maria Serena, against its steep mountain backdrop (facing pag[e]*

part is now carpeted with dense *garrigue* vegetation: box, myrtle, laurustinus, among which stand giant agaves.

Part of this median strip was transformed between the wars into a private garden, full of mock medieval ruins. As its owner was regularly strapped for funds, the vicomte de Noailles regularly bought it up and sold it back as the man's fortunes fluctuated—an original way of helping out a neighbor!

The city of Hyères is converting the entire hillside into one large public park to be called Le Jardin Provençal. The Castel Sainte-Claire (three acres in size) will remain a brightly flowered, exotic domain where rare specimens, such as bauhinias and erythrinas, stand among patterned bedding plants, gay lantanas, sages, oleanders and abutilons. Its general style recalls the public garden-landscape park tradition of the late nineteenth century: palm trees set in lawns with circles of multicolored flowers, in wedges, at their feet.

The six-acre park of the Villa Noailles will continue to specialize in Mediterranean plants. The soil here is not deep—as little as fifty centimeters in some places. And although the house was designed with twenty bathrooms, much used thanks to a passion for sports and physical fitness which Marie-Laure de Noailles imposed on all her guests, water is now scarce. The plants which have survived and those planted today tend to be drought-resistant. There are, for example, some twenty varieties of rosemary, fifteen of phlomis, and twenty-five different cistus.

The entire hillside is thus undergoing transformations at present. But visitors to the Villa Noailles may already discover a magic world of colorful bloom combining both usual and rare plants, laid out below the house on a series of terraces. The original olive trees and one magnificent three hundred-year-old almond tree provide a solid structure. At the heart of the hillside stand three enormous parasol pines, flanked by a clump of cypresses to the east, a dramatic focal point in the middle ground between house and village beyond. The protected site allows for winter-flowering buddlejas (*B. officinalis* and *B. madagascariensis*, both favorites of the vicomte). There are red passion flowers tumbling over a balustrade, white-flowered *Beaumontia*, and hundreds of pink biennial echiums which self-sow, and reach up to three meters tall. Design here is less formal than in the neighboring Castel, though plants are still grouped in spreads of vibrant color—yellow phlomis running among massed dimorphothecas and lantanas, for example. Paths often run along the outer edges of the terraces, whose proportions and generally rectangular shape are respected. Individual terraces have developed different characters according to their plantations.

These central terraces are enclosed on either side by old stone walls. On the middle levels, arches open onto sheltered secret gardens: to the west is the walled *enclos* in front of the guest house lent to composer Georges Auric, a long, narrow promenade with large beds of mixed, low shrubs and perennials spreading under olive and almond crowns. To the east, a high staircase leads down to

Gabriel Guévrékian's cubist garden was created to extend Robert Mallet-Steven's villa in the 1920s, when avant-garde artists of all kinds flocked to the Villa Noailles in Hyères. Today this triangle seems dull compared to the inventive profusion of the lower gardens.

intimate, semi-formal beds on several levels, their paths paved with terracotta tiles.

Decorative effect is the first aim of this garden, however many rare finds may be tucked into corners. Even very simple groupings are quite appealing: *Cistus corbariensis*, for example, with its reddish buds, mingled with sages, echiums, lavenders, and pink-flowered phlomis. Deep blue-green echium, smaller in volume than the more gray-blue varieties, combines in one place with pink phlomis, in another with polygala and yellow phlomis, or with a deep cerise wall flower.

These plantings are the work of Pierre Quillier, grandson of the vicomte's former intendant. Quillier grew up on this property where his grandfather still lives in a house bequeathed to him at the vicomte's death. No gardener could be more in love with his charge. The Villa Noailles has been blessed with great good luck in having him. He is working both to restore the collections and strengthen the design. He seeks out new items not for their rarity but for their strong flowering, or their powerful fragrance. Quillier also planned a pattern of blue agapanthus and yellow coreopsis under the giant parasol pines which frame the view of the town from the house. This design discreetly echoes the cubist design above and connects the trees to the more informal garden beyond. It is he who collected the biennial echiums and made sure they would prosper all over the hillside.

This famous property is both enchanted and enchanting. Now it no longer lives in the shadow of former brilliance but has begun a new life of its own.

LA CHEVRE D'OR

It is difficult, perhaps, for the public to realize the immense problems facing any individual or group wanting to restore or maintain such elaborate gardens today. Many were highly personal creations, like the Villa Roquebrune, where only the owner really knew the extent and variety of the treasures contained therein—and the individual care each requires. Municipal gardeners are not trained for such specialized upkeep, and tend to prune hard rare specimens, or set out bedding plants for instant color with sometimes disastrous effects, like the dread oxalis which later smothers everything in sight. Family members who inherit such paradises may find their lives entirely changed by the event—as in the case of William Waterfield, who has made his life around the Clos du Peyronnet, but wonders about the next generation.

Another splendid and very famous garden is now hanging fire in just this manner, now that both its original creators have passed on. This is the much-photographed Chèvre d'Or near Biot, developed in the 1950s from an old rural domain.

The Chèvre d'Or began with a legend: buried treasure at the foot of a Romanesque tower which still stands at the road outside the gate. The owners of the property, Monsieur and Madame Champin, first enlarged the villa, consolidated its terraces, and planted a garden for the summer months only. Intimate patios, some paved with patterned pebbles, surround the house, sheltering pots of fragrant plants—cestrums, pelargoniums, frangipani. From here one can see the imposing and very famous perspective of the green garden, where low hedges of box, rosemary, and myrtle curve around an avenue of Italian jars containing orange tree globes, the avenue now somewhat overshadowed by the giant cypress curtain opposite. The Chèvre d'Or is again a garden of friendship: such famous gardeners as Basil Leng, the duchesse de Mouchy, the vicomte de Noailles, the princesse Sturdza, the baronne de Waldner and Sir Peter Smithers all contributed advice and plants. The most celebrated corners of the Chèvre d'Or include a monumental cypress lane planted on ground rising away from the house, for greater effect; a ceanothus garden; a Japanese corner with standard trained wisterias and a checkerboard of green and silver santolinas; the pleached olive hedge, underplanted with box, which leads to the elegant *Orangerie*; white and pink gardens; the sundial surrounded by balls of rhaphiolepis. Will all these treasures, so often described and photographed, survive the transition? Or will one of the most original gardens of the French Riviera be lost to posterity?

The gardens at the Villa Noailles in Grasse contain many travel memories and echoes, like this reproduction in miniature of the famous Aldobrandini column near Rome (center).

THE VILLA NOAILLES AT GRASSE

Another great postwar property, the Villa Noailles at Grasse, experienced a similar period of dangerous indecision before being taken in hand by the vicomte's grandson, aided by landscaper-in-residence Jane Harvey.

While his wife continued to preside over the brilliant world of their villa in Hyères, the vicomte de Noailles sought out a more peaceful existence in the backcountry near Grasse. His garden there became legendary in its own right, and has probably proven more seminal than any other of that period.

The long-abandoned, eighteenth-century villa with its steep, olive-planted hillside was bought at auction before World War II by the vicomte de Noailles. This man, who has been warmly commended by all who knew him for "impeccable taste, incomparable imagination and boundless generosity," created between 1947 and his death in 1981 a garden which Roderick Cameron described as "the ideal garden" for the French Riviera.

And yet, like Lawrence Johnston's Serre de la Madone, it has no sea view. Perhaps its self-containment was part of the appeal for the vicomte, for whom the panorama at Hyères was all too familiar. And while the latter was militantly avant-garde, the domain at Grasse has a timeless quality: it is ancient, even Virgilian in its muted tones and pastoral echoes. It is modern, however, in its inventive use of garden traditions, and in its balance between rich plant collections and strong design.

Water spirits inhabit this garden in all of its parts, from the mossy spring in the lime tree-shaded courtyard as one enters, to the series of fountains and basins which accompany the descent to the moist meadow below. There are deliberate allusions to the Villa d'Este, and a half-sized reproduction of the famous Roman torsaded Aldobrandini column. For this, too, is a garden of travel memories and echoes. The villa itself presides at the upper, northeast corner of the property. The visitor, coming in through the courtyard behind, with its famous tiered pots of camellias and lichenous statues in niches, can continue along the back wall, past the Italianate *buffet d'eau*. A trellis supporting Banksia roses leads to the famous pergola of Judas trees where, on the advice of the landscaper Russell Page, every fifth one flowered white.

Below, immediately west of the house, a series of small terraces extends in long strips. Curiously, the dwelling has no direct or obvious connection with the garden, no formal point of entry. The passage from the courtyard is softly modulated with the help of two semi-circular stone flights of steps. A pair of gentle, somewhat bemused stone lions welcome and guide the visitor through this transition toward a spread of emerald lawn. This in turn stretches toward a majestic horse chestnut, whose billowing crown echoes the soft lines of the hills beyond.

On the terrace below, which appears sunken due to its high, dark ramparts of yew, is the collection of rare peonies, leading to the Aldobrandini column at its west end. The fountain stands out against the blue-gray curtain of a glaucous cypress backed by a stand of Judas trees.

At the east end of this peony garden, close to the house, a stand of boxwood has been

Close to the house, a tall, sculpted boxwood pavilion rises from a froth of silver santolina (facing page).

sculpted into a high, dark pavilion which dominates a froth of santolina at its feet. One of the most imposing features of garden architecture on the Riviera, this box pavilion forms a sort of triumphal arch, through which one may return to the house at its lowest level.

Designed by architect Emilio Terry, the lower and south-facing patio is also surrounded by sculpted box hedging, here kept low enough to anchor two giant cypresses, and help them frame the distant view—hilltop after hilltop, fading into blue distance. Set into the house itself is a tiled alcove which invites restful admiration of the prospect beyond. Perfumed *Akebia quinata* and *Holboellia latifolia* climb over it. In the center of this patio is a simple, round basin with pots of lilies round its rim. Monsieur de Noailles stocked it with pink and white Japanese carp.

So it is that the spaces around the house have been transformed into an intricate series of separate garden rooms, interconnected in surprising ways, each with its special—and by now celebrated—character. But this is only the domain's upper northeast corner. The general plan of the rest is easy to grasp—although still full of secret nooks to discover, many set at the far (west) end where a winding path descends.

The garden's heart remains a series of seven broad, stone-walled terraces supporting ancient olive trees. Wild and rare bulbs (among them narcissi, crocuses, fritillaries, and anemones) turn these spaces to white, gold, or pink carpets at different times of year. In Monsieur de Noailles's time, the grass was left uncut until summer, but mown

paths zigzagged among them. In the beginning, he let his tenant farmer graze sheep here, which he found decorative, but this nearly proved fatal to the bulbs so the practice had to be stopped.

Set on the outer edge of the lowest terrace is a large, rectangular basin edged with weathered stone. A clump of *Beschorneria yuccoides*, that architectural plant with huge tufts of sword-like leaves and coral-red spears of flowers, sits along the basin's north side, and indeed similar clumps punctuate the olive terraces all up and down the hillside. This reservoir looks down on a fresh strip of manicured, emerald lawn, a striking contrast to the wild grass above. Plans are afoot to enhance the rectangular lawn with formal parterres: a design of large, medium, and small box balls, with a row of summer-flowering *Koelreuteria paniculata* along the outer edge. A flagstone path already leads to an elegant, tiled pavilion.

One of this garden's best effects is its alternation of rural simplicity with such touches of formal refinement. There are similar constructions, small loggias and summer houses in pale pink, sometimes with white columns, always with benches, hidden at different points on the hillside.

Indeed, points of repose are everywhere, allowing admiration of the garden from many angles. For while the distant view appeals with its soft curves, the hills behind rise high enough to enhance the sense of enclosure which makes this garden such a haven.

The soft gray stone retaining walls which support the broad olive terraces at the heart of the garden do not extend in a straight line nor even a curve across the hillside, but make an oblique angle at one point, dividing the hill asymmetrically in two. The strong rhythm thus created is enhanced by a long flight of wide stone steps, a vertical axis down the east edge of these terraces—nothing elaborate but, on the contrary, a sort of donkey track with an ivy-covered balustrade. At its foot, now in the lower middle of the hillside, stands a stone pyramid from Napoleonic times, flanked by a dusty-pink clump of pampas grass, more *Beschorneria*, and a rare yucca-like plant (*Hesperaloe passiflora* var. *englemanii*). These commanding shapes mark one of the garden's main focal points, softened by the surrounding small garden build-

easy access up and down the middle of the hillside, the visitor's promenade often runs along the north and west edges of the property, which afford an entirely different series of perspectives. Starting again from the house, one passes through a densely shaded laurel walk at the very top of the hill (where sheets of marble-leaved cyclamen magically carpet the ground). The winding descent along the west boundary reveals in turn a pavilion carved from bay laurel behind an octagonal pool, another aviary, a small terrace formally planted with squares of different ground cover plants around a sculpted pillar of carnival masks, an extensively-trellised wisteria sheltering rare camellias, a formal arrangement of aromatic plants, and

The Noailles gardens in Grasse celebrate water in every corner, as refreshing to the ear as it is to the eye. This fountain stands on a lower terrace against the flowering trees of the meadow below. Viewed from below, the fountain helps frame the house in a long perspective from the other side of the garden.

ings (one sporting a celebrated faun's head fountain made of white marble), and groups of rare, fragrant shrubs including apricot-scented *Osmanthus fragrans aurantiacus*. Here, set off by a panel of Delft tiles, stood Monsieur de Noailles's main aviary.

At the slope's lower limit extends the meadow with its inimitable groves of magnolias and Japanese cherries, including a *Halesia carolina* or snowdrop tree. The whole, a mass of pale billowing bloom in early spring, was once thickly underplanted with sheets of camassias, wild gladiolas and *Lilium monadelphum*. The trees have been grouped and planned for successive flowering. In the bottom corner stands the collector's pride: a giant, *Metasequoia glyptostroboides*.

Although the donkey track steps offer

twin Russian olives (or oleasters, *Eleagnus angustifolia*) whose falling silver foliage is reflected in a round pool. A camphor tree has now replaced the famous *Magnolia campbellii mollicomata* nearby. Below, a collection of camellias is screened by a blowsy terracotta bust of a woman by Carrier-Belleuse. A beautiful calm rectangular pool edged with arum lilies lies hidden on this level. Just below this lies the famous mandrake root, which Monsieur de Noailles ("with a certain Puckish humour," says Roderick Cameron) once depicted on Christmas cards. And finally, the tree-planted meadow, where stone-edged canals make elegant lines among the magnolias and Japanese cherries.

From this southwest corner, one can look back at the house diagonally opposite, past the pyramid and a series of punctuating fountains. Certain effects of this perspective have been attenuated and blurred by rampant tree growth since the vicomte's time, but restoration will soon re-establish them.

The east edge of the property below the house has yet more treasures: a rockery with an ingenious bamboo watering system, the gardener's house, another camellia collection, and a series of informally planted terraces with rare shrubs and small trees, situated below a picturesque gargoyle drainspout. Here one finds a silver and gold garden, including a yellow-flowering horse chestnut tree, whose crown grows tall enough to frame a stone bench just below the house.

Throughout the vicomte's lifetime, the

may be necessary. Certainly this elaborate garden, with its soft lines and gentle transitions, its musical fountains, its witty use of open and closed, large and small spaces, could well become a haven in high summer as well as a delight in early spring.

Such are the gardens which constitute the core of the Riviera legend in its gardening dimension, those which have provided models for following generations. And such are the problems arising from their maintenance or lack or it, demise or rebirth. Many of these domains can be glimpsed at an earlier stage in the photographs of the vicomte de Noailles's book (written in collaboration with Roy Lancaster), *Plantes de jardins méditerranéens* published in 1977. Indeed, the authors' sensi-

The vicomte ...ailles's great joy ...his collection of ...olias, flowering ...ies, and still more ...ual spring- ...ning trees spread ...n the moist bottom ...ow, underplanted ...bulbs. The meadow ...w being restored ...would have wished.

gardens were open to the public. Local people came for Sunday walks, and many had their wedding pictures taken there. Gardeners of all kinds and ambitions found it a continuing source of inspiration. Plantings peaked in early spring, although Monsieur de Noailles did allow spots of oleander and lagerstroemia so that the later months would not be entirely devoid of color. Now the Villa Noailles has opened its gates to the public once again, under special conditions, and it is expected that most visitors will come in summer. As a result, experiments are being made with collections of salvias and other reliable summer-blooming plants—an effective blending, for example, of *Salvia uliginosa*, golden day lilies, and nandina. Monsieur de Noailles loved muted colors, but here too adjustments

tive presentation of the gardens of that time in their introduction makes this work a precious documentation of much that has already disappeared. Most of the gardens cited are along the way to becoming historical monuments, their fame recognized and acknowledged as part of a public patrimony.

French Riviera garden owners today, whether of grand or modest circumstances, look to this golden past for inspiration and information. The contemporary range is just as broad but the emphasis has changed. By far the great majority of Côte d'Azur gardens are now situated on backcountry hillsides, and the variety of treatments imagined for such sites is proof in itself that the old challenge of personal fancy passionately pursued continues to thrive.

Today's fashion in Riviera gardening follows the vicomte de Noailles's example in seeking the rustic refinement of terraced hillsides (following pages).

Terraces
in the Sun

Contemporary gardeners on the French Riviera tend to abandon the famous coastline between Menton and Antibes, now often cluttered and congested, and take to the hills. The back-country between Grasse and Nice has proven particularly attractive, thanks to such factors as the success of the Riviera's "think tank," Sophia Antipolis, a proliferation of golf courses, and the development of fast connections by road. The vista from the highway linking Grasse to Le Rouret has become one of the most sought after, a kind of "little Tuscany," where the planting of cypress trees in the foreground deliberately evokes the Italian region. Not that these slopes were empty before the current trend, however: inland properties were already popular between the wars, when British novelist Ford Madox Ford wrote that "every monticule behind the narrow strip of littoral is crowned with an agreeable villa, having shady and brilliant-flowered gardens." Now these older domains are much sought-after as the point of departure for new fashions: the quiet, rural elegance which has taken root as the new Riviera style.

The variety of gardens to be discovered on terraced Riviera hillsides provides unending pleasure and astonishment for the garden observer. Some have been created by talented designers of international reputation, others by retired couples of limited means, still others by wealthy industrialists creating their dream gardens. Artists and writers seem to have a special affinity for these dramatic sites. Renoir bought his six-acre property at Cagnes-sur-Mer in 1906 to save a splendid olive orchard from destruction. The house he built near the old farm of Les Colettes looks down on an old-fashioned, tiered garden of citrus and roses. He particularly loved the way olive foliage changes with the weather. In his correspondence, he described it as "sad under gray skies, sonorous in the sunlight, silvery in the wind."

The following descriptions—a kind of sampling—illustrate the extreme range of ingenious adaptations to the site to be found in little-known Riviera domains. Each has a similar point of departure in this strongly architectural setting, where stone and vegetation inevitably mix; but each of the gardens which result from it is absolutely unique. Other examples can be found in other chapters, since indeed the majority of Côte d'Azur properties are thus situated.

Lawrence Johnston and the vicomte de Noailles, creators of early, legendary Riviera gardens, were virtuosi in the genre of terraced hillsides, impressive pathfinders for future generations. Both of their gardens were self-contained, however. Today's owners generally prefer sites with a prospect, often the Mediterranean itself scintillating in the distance beyond layer upon layer of hills. Film star Dirk Bogarde remembers walking among his four hundred olive trees on terraces near Cabris, "through drifts of wild anemones . . . the sea shining like a silver knife thrusting from the Estérel mountains."

Such terraced orchards of olive trees in rough grass are naturally carpeted with wild bulbs in spring and fall. A newcomer to the

*S*tone walls
create wonderful visual
rhythms from all angles.
Here their tiered lines
are seen from below,
past a magnolia at the
Villa Noailles.

area, Lady Fortescue, laboriously set out a few expensive samples imported from Holland in the 1950s. She recounts the experience in her popular book *Perfume from Provence*. "When spring burst upon us one perfect morning, I found the grassy terraces under the olive-trees one sheet of tiny blue Roman hyacinths, miniature scarlet tulips, mauve and scarlet anemones, and yellow jonquils. When I exclaimed in delight to Hilaire [her local gardener] that our predecessor here had planted lavishly and beautifully, he at first looked blank, and then, when I pointed rapturously to the jewelled grass on the terraces below, he gave one contemptuous glance and said, 'Ah ça!—sont sauvages, Madame.'"

English landscape architect Russell Page, more knowledgeable, took his cue from nature in dealing with these sites. In his book *Education of a Gardener*, he writes about them with obvious appreciation: "I have very often gardened in Mediterranean places where old olive trees gave the basic note with their gnarled and twisted trunks and silvery-grey, sun-flecked foliage. These are patient trees which will live two thousand years in the stoniest ground. On the outskirts of the garden *Iris unguicularis* can be naturalised under them as well as freesia and the wild scarlet and blue anemones, small white Roman hyacinths and the white jonquils for their scent." For a garden with such a rustic style, he recommended underplantings of lawn closer to the house, with colorful climbers in the branches: mauve wisteria, blue kennedya, yellow and white Banksia roses, *Rosa anemonoides*, and 'La Follette'.

Page did not invent the idea of rambling roses threading their way through high crowns of silvery foliage. Lady Fortescue also admired giant, pale yellow Banksia roses among the olive trees, "rioting all over them, cascading and dripping from the gnarled branches at the very top." Banksia and the 'La Follette' have been widely used in this manner for decades. It is said that the latter became popular on the trellises of cafés and bistrots because of its exuberant growth, before being promoted as a garden ornament by the Schneider sisters at their influential nursery in Cannes.

Many cosmopolitan owners regard such rustic décors with frank nostalgia for old country ways. Lady Fortescue much admired one Pierre, a beekeeper, who "finds happiness pottering among his flowers, his fruit-trees, his few vegetables, his bees, and his birds. . . . He sweeps a brawny arm out towards the majesty of mountains rising above a sea of grey-green olive foliage, and asks me why people spend their lives striving to make money when *le bon Dieu* gives them all this beauty for nothing?"

Lady Fortescue's version may be a mite sentimental, and such vast vistas, nowadays, are rarely free. But the dream she cultivated has seduced the most sophisticated, and the terraced olive plantation has remained at its heart. Perhaps as an antidote to the stresses of the worldly life? Bogarde recalls a television producer friend who, every time he had to go to London to do one of his shows, "was in such despair at leaving that he would walk round his garden embracing every olive tree."

As vestiges of an appealing rural past, terraced olive plantations survive unchanged in surprising places. Between Cannes and the backcountry some forty miles distant lies a stretch of road particularly well-known for its traffic snarls and slowdowns. Unremarked by passing motorists, an elegant wrought-iron gate admits entrance not only to a private domain, but to another century. The lane moves up through the classic, layered site with its ancient, gnarled trunks. In the spring, the grass at their feet is bejeweled with anemones, narcissi, vetches, orchids, wild bulbs, and flowers of every color and description. The ocher-toned house is flanked by giant cypress sentinels. The garden is simple and traditional: a shaded courtyard, pots around a faun's head fountain. A shepherd still grazes his flock on the wilder reaches above the house, and local people come hunting wild asparagus. The caretaker, originally from Piedmont and once a truck farmer on this very land, meticulously prunes the olive trees, branch by branch, in the early spring, his weather-lined face a portrait of the land itself.

Such oases are prized as remnants, however besieged, of an earthy vitality which is today at a premium. Current owners all speak with pride of pressing their own olives for oil, and most have a vegetable plot tucked away somewhere on the property. But nostalgia does not prevent the development of such sites for highly modern décors—as a setting for displays of contemporary sculpture, for example. Each gardener inevitably creates a paradise in his or her own image.

BASTIDE GARDENS

The traditional gardens of terraced Riviera backcountry were those which surrounded aristocratic country residences, whose owners spent their summers in the country, their winters in town. Loosely termed *bastides* (a name less clearly defined in this region than around Aix and Marseille further west), they still exist in quantity. Grasse's most elegant domains are situated in the hamlets which surround the town, each with a different saint's name—refined seventeenth- and eighteenth-century properties built when the city was achieving international fame for its perfumes. The houses, not châteaux but larger and more imposing versions of the local farmsteads, snuggle against the hillside, facing south or southeast, sheltered in summer by carefully pruned canopies of lime trees or mulberries or chestnuts (more common than planes in this area). Several such giant parasols are generally needed to shade the length of the extensive building. In front of the house, beneath the trees, extends the broadest, flattest expanse of the garden, a terrace at least partially paved, often giving onto a panoramic view as far as the sea.

Carved stone balustrades, benches, and fountains underscore the Italianate design of these properties, which may also contain small, ornamental pavilions, elaborate pergolas, and stone-edged basins. Formal parterres are rare, though in one unusual valley site below Grasse, once inhabited by Romans and now surrounded by golf greens, an entire boxwood labyrinth was laid out in the nineteenth century. Another example dates from the 1920s, when fashionable architect J.C.N. Forestier designed colorful floral parterres for the princesse de Polignac at the Bastide du Roy near Biot. Into these formal patterns, he ingeniously integrated a whole orchard of imposing but irregularly-spaced olive trees.

Usually a steep hillside below the *bastide* precludes much horizontal display. Like the rise above, which protects the house, it will be terraced. The high crowns of its olive trees are everywhere set off by clipped greenery—cypress columns, or stone steps accompanied by rounded box balls, or retaining walls smothered in carefully contained ivy. Roses, wisteria, coronillas, and Judas trees provide single notes of color against the green, as do glazed or unglazed pots for summer flowers. Contemporary owners often enrich this floral display. But the lines of the terrace walls, along with the massive olive trees and their companion cypresses, still dominate the scene.

Access to the traditional *bastide* starts with a stone-pillared, wrought-iron gate, zigzags along these tiers, and arrives alongside the building from above or below, depending on the site.

Sometimes terraces just above and below the house have been converted (even very recently) into a formal garden itinerary, with more pools, paving, and pergolas, while the upper and lower reaches retain their agricultural character. It is on the more distant levels that extensive kitchen plots were once cultivated, the olive trees tended for oil production. Celebrated Riviera chef Jacques Chibois, now converting the splendid Bastide de Saint-Antoine just outside Grasse into a rustic but sophisticated restaurant, hopes to revive its vegetable gardens. Diners will be able to taste the results in the *bastide*'s courtyard, next to the old well decked with ivy and white wreaths of *Clematis armandii*, or the unusual, red trumpet-flowered bignonia flanked by a purple bougainvillea on the ocher façade.

Another elegant *bastide* garden near Hyères has a most original agricultural setting: a former watercress plantation! Needless to say, water is plentiful here, and carved fountains abound on every level. These are further linked by stone canals running along both sides of the long steps which descend the hillside, enclosed at first by a tunnel of enormous oleanders, later by an olive tree lane. Today this property hangs between restoration of its rich heritage and the innovations of an owner passionate about plants, who is improving the garden's texture with a great variety of new trees and shrubs. In a few years, this may become one of the most fascinating Riviera gardens. At the moment, its charm is the somewhat Romantic appeal of old-fashioned, overgrown domains. Its outlying fields are still cultivated and here

provide a stunning display of artichokes, there leeks lined up like soldiers, and elsewhere, arum lilies.

Many such country properties, which look age-old, have in fact been redesigned by contemporary, often cosmopolitan landscapers. The properties' elegance depends on a sophisticated imitation of rural tradition. Thus an Italianate domain near Grasse was first transformed from a local farmhouse by an English painter in the 1920s, and its impressive reception rooms were in fact once his studio. The beautifully proportioned steps leading to the lower esplanade are the work of architect Emilio Terry. The intricately carved stone entrance doorframe was brought from the region of Aix-en-Provence. Although everything here blends harmoniously, the garden's elements belie an eclectic internationalism which remains always the first characteristic of Riviera style.

Among the many ocher-washed *bastides* west of Grasse, one was redesigned some fifty years ago in a style which mixes Italianate elements and romantic meanderings, even fragments of Gothic ruins. The long house façade has two asymmetrical turrets, and its warmth is complemented by deep blue turquoise shutters. All of the windows have been framed by a carefully pruned wisteria which has covered the whole façade and become an extraordinary element of the architecture itself. The customary shade trees of the broad terrace, here two tall limes, have been shaped by an equally gifted hand into a lacework pattern of curves and nodes

Near Grasse, skillful prun creates such marvels this façade outlined wisteria (facing pag

Fifty years ago, a gardener near Grasse created this imaginative series of formal garden rooms, their rigor softened by the billowing purple crowns of Judas trees (below).

A carved stone balustrade ma the lower limit of the Grasse garden witho separating it from the landscape beyon its natural, wilder extension (following pages).

East of the Grasse bastide lies an intimate garden around a refreshing pool with an ivy-covered pavilion (above). A path down from the Grasse bastide, bright with coronilla, leads toward the vegetable plot (center).

which stand dramatically against the early spring sky. Below them, stone snakes entwined around a pair of mossy urns guard the levels below.

This general prospect opens onto the surrounding valley, beautifully displayed between the limits of green hedges on either side, and the less manicured stretches of formerly cultivated olive tree terracing beyond. Water lies at the heart of this garden: from the house, a series of three basins descends from level to level, reached by straight and twin-ramped stone staircases. A fourth basin, in fact an agricultural reservoir, adds its mirror surface to the series, below an elegantly carved stone balustrade running across the hillside, the line strengthened further by poplar and cypress towers. The great originality of this sequence is that the axis is not straight, but goes charmingly askew as it descends.

Each of the broad green terraces extending on each level of the descent has its own character and special features: one leads to a fragment of Gothic arches outlined by a green ivy square, their ogives framing pale mauve iris beds; another to a row of particularly beautiful, soaring lagerstroemia with their mottled beige and silver bark and colorful late bloom, beyond which steps descend

toward a hidden fountain. More paths move onward from here to a cherub statue guarding an ivy-covered pavilion, and still further on, to the vegetable garden.

On the third level of the main descent, pointed box domes some two meters high, arranged like so many soldiers in military formation, gather around a central, ivy-decked stone pedestal with carved masks. At the east end of this terrace, a squared-off cypress hedge hides yet another garden room, sheltering citrus trees.

Around such formal elements, the plantings remain soft and rustic—one particularly well-placed tamarisk provides just the right focal point over a long period in spring, while Judas crowns punctuate the greenery with mauve, as they always do in gardens of this style. The trees look particularly effective framing a geometric parterre east of the house, where tiered topiary shelters another large, stone-edged basin, slightly sunken, fronted by a row of gnarled and spreading olive trees.

This is the traditional Provençal garden reworked for more elaborate display, more theatrical effect, but it has retained its familiar homey atmosphere.

A garden designed by Russell Page, Castel Mougins, has much clearer, cleaner lines, sparse and austere in comparison. It was first

laid out some forty years ago and is no doubt the best surviving example of this celebrated landscaper's work on the French Riviera. Set just under the crest of a hilltop, it has perhaps the most stunning panoramic view of any garden in the area, extending from Grasse and the Alps to the broad sweep of the Mediterranean, intercepted by the towers of a picturesque hilltown nearby. Its best features are already famous: the elegantly curving, raised beds leading from the wrought-iron entrance gate to the house under pine canopies; the circular pool of the *cour d'honneur*; the strong, central axis which penetrates the house before continuing down the terraced hillside; the three formal parterres laid out in rectangles with their citrus globes and their yellow and blue tulips (of different heights) encased in low euonymus hedges; the baroque staircase descent to broad olive terraces, originally underplanted with drifts of agapanthus, *Amaryllis belladonna*, narcissi, irises, Japanese anemones, and echiums. The present owner has made some additions that strengthen still further the spirit of the original conception. Indeed, she says, Page himself approved them and told her this was his favorite garden in the region.

Page's design stopped below the house with the olive tree terraces, where the strong lines of the old retaining walls converge gracefully in a columned flight of steps. Today's owner has simply planted the lower reaches (still expanses of wild, mown grass) with rigorous lines of mimosa also clipped into globes. The mimosa's feathery, dark green foliage echoes the similar shape and size of olive crowns. Together with the citrus balls closer to the house, the elements create a pleasing three-tiered effect. Tall pines, a cypress pillar and the rounded canopies of old Judas trees sheltering the house soften the composition's formal geometries.

The perspective from the house has thus been lengthened but remains simple, in keeping with one of Page's favorite tenets: a spectacular view must be framed but not undermined. At the same time, the prospect looking back from the lower, eastern limit of the garden allows for fresh discovery of the whole sequence from a different angle. The swimming pool, with its elegant, colonnaded pavilion, provides an enjoyable vantage point.

This is a very controlled garden, where pruning, says the owner, is never severe enough. It still uses bedding annuals in the grand tradition, in whites and greens (2200

Bastide
gardens today still use
clipped greenery
(rosemary, box, and
cypress) as a foil
for fanciful sculpture,
like these sea monsters
(below) or the two
musical bears (facing
page).

petunia plants through the winter). The best architectural elements were brought by the original restorer, the marquis de Ronalle, from the Aix area, in keeping with the majestic character of the site and his interpretation of it. And since stone columns are one of the themes of the property, today's owner has also extended the building at each end with colonnaded winter garden areas (partly enclosed by glass), once again paying such strict attention to proportion that she calculated their girth to the exact millimeter. She has kept, however, the informal groves of flowering shrubs and fruiting trees with which Page originally softened these transitions between house and garden.

Thus Castel Mougins, remnant of a distinguished past, continues to live and evolve. It is still in superb form.

SCULPTURE GARDENS

Most of the old *bastide* gardens still contain good sculpture in one form or another—sometimes animating a fountain, sometimes as familiar spirits presiding amid the greenery. East of Grasse, an elegant, eighteenth-century domain, including vines and olive plantations, lies on fifteen acres of hillside. The beautiful façade is set off by the twining, thick trunks of old vines which shade the door. In a sheltered corner against the east side of the house stands a lovely fountain, surrounded by pots in a decorative array. In front of the house, on the far right corner of its stone-paved terrace, a small outdoor room

has been created under a roof of dense trelliswork, with a vantage point on the entire garden below. A rococo sculpture of a dog in human dress graciously invites entrance.

This property's most striking feature is a vertical axis which descends the hillside, a double lane of cypresses flanking a cascade of water caught in a series of small basins halfway down the slope. From the house terrace, the point of departure of this dramatic descent is guarded by two stone bears, each different, each expressive.

In an even more secluded backcountry domain nearby, other appealing creatures watch over a stone-edged basin: two sea monsters recline along its west side as if sunbathing, each with a different, comical expression. The pool is reached through a cobbled courtyard with an arched entrance half-smothered in ivy. At the far end, this terrace looks out at one of the most dramatically perched hilltowns of the area. This *bastide* has also kept terraced olive plantations of considerable age on its lower slopes.

The atmosphere can be so strong in these old-fashioned properties that one can almost feel them inhabited by nature spirits, as the Romans believed about their gardens. Their sculptured personages are powerful presences indeed.

Some adaptations of old rural properties transform the sites into theatrical settings for modern sculpture. An eleventh-century abbey near Vence has thus been converted into a perfume museum overlooking a display of contemporary sculpture on several levels.

Adrien
Maeght's private gar
perpetuates the rustic
Provençal traditions
but his pool reflects t
imaginative forms
of a Léger mosaic
(following pages).

oaring pines at the Fondation Maeght at Saint-Paul-de-Vence provide an idyllic setting for the sculpture collections, including Miró's expressive birds.

This domain is known poetically as Château Notre-Dame-des-Fleurs. It is now being transformed into an art gallery.

No doubt the most celebrated sculpture garden of the region is the Fondation Maeght at Saint-Paul. It was created, also in the early 1960s, by art book publishers Marguerite and Aimé Maeght, around a contemporary building of architect José-Luis Sert. But the private garden of their son, Adrien Maeght, who still directs the family gallery in Paris, was conceived on successive levels around an old country house. Here too, pines and shrubbery set off a pool with a mosaic signed by Fernand Léger, and other, similarly impressive works of art serve as focal points in the garden.

The private Maeght garden is in fact many in one. The house sits at the center and each surrounding wedge of the hillside has a different character. The shadowy pinewood, sheltering giant sculptures, provides an extreme contrast with a broad wedge of spiky succulents baking in the sun to the west. Much of the hilltop is now given over to a giant rockery, where brilliant flowers (delospermas, gazanias, echiums) find sustenance among rough stone. But the overall mood of the property is still one of rural simplicity. The strong lines of a pergola, built with squared stone pillars, descend from the house to terraces planted with vegetables, fruit and olive orchards, and vineyards, of which Adrien Maeght is particularly proud. This is still a country retreat, though one may pass a massive Miró sculpture as one goes to pick salad.

A LABYRINTH GARDEN

One of the most unusual sculpture gardens of the region owes much to the southern tradition of clipped greenery acting as a décor for statuary, although here human and animal forms give way to abstract geometry. This witty and somewhat theatrical creation, a particularly personal and very avant-garde blend, was imagined by two well-known contemporary sculptors, Robert Courtright and Bruno Romeda. They treat stone, metal, wood, and vegetation as complementary materials for their art. This domain excels at framing, enclosing, exposing, hiding, and surprising, and its labyrinthine design is truly a delight.

Here the olive tree terraces occupy a triangular plot of only two acres. From the gate, a long driveway leads toward the house. On the steep hillside above it, retaining walls support bands of santolinas, vines, iris, and tumbling rosemary in tiers of contrasting color and texture, so that the flat spaces between are foreshortened, invisible. At the top, groves of cypress and olive trees hide the artists' studio, though its intricate trelliswork may be glimpsed through the foliage.

Approaching the house along the driveway, one sees directly ahead an arch linking the house to the high wall which surrounds its patio. Ivy runs from the tall chimney of the house, over the arch, and along the wall beyond, making a continuous, flat surface, a first example of this garden's intimate links between constructed elements and vegetation. Just before reaching this gate, however,

one discovers on the left a surprising series of tiny terraces, rising beneath the stiff canopy of a loquat tree. Here a line of miniature box domes alternates with silver-feathered cineraria—a jewel-box of a garden. Weather-worn stone steps lead upward past this display to a junction of hedges and olive foliage floating above multiple trunks, suggesting a number of possible directions beyond.

But first the most intimate space of the garden must be explored: the enclosed courtyard behind the ivy-draped arch. Set against the south façade of the house, it is sheltered by high walls east and west. Opposite, however, only a low wall (again, ivy covered) separates it from the old olive terraces, so that their silvery crowns can be fully appreciated from above.

This patio is small, but full of intricately echoing forms: box balls in glazed pots, citrus globes against the house, fragrant star jasmine tumbling over the walls near the rounded arches (opening east as well as west). The paving has been laid on two slightly different levels, using old earthenware tiles and stone with much the same colors. Stone, earth, and vegetation share the complicity of the circle—repeated in metal in one of Bruno Romeda's graceful bronze rings (entitled *Cerchi*) on a raised dais in one corner.

The eastern passage through the courtyard wall leads to a series of broader terraces outside, some revealing the valley view and orchards at the bottom of the hillside, others enclosed in various ways: by blocked-off hedges, or clumps of trees such as almonds. Most of the shapes on this series of terraces

are squares and cubes. On a top level near the house, the back wall is punctuated with square terracotta planters containing box cubes—a nice contrast of orange and dark green. At the end of another terrace, six squared-off cypresses frame two rough and wizened stone troughs, which support a regiment of green glazed pots. Another loquat, with its strongly architectural foliage, shades the scene.

Certainly the most subtle surprise of this part of the garden is the framing of a multi-branching olive trunk by one of Romeda's large, bronze triangles. Through the sculpture, one sees close by the tree's limbs beginning to spread, an upside-down triangular shape. From this particular vantage point, two triangles are thus visually superimposed: Romeda's upright, the tree's with its point toward the ground. The metallic, man-made form echoes and inverts the natural creation.

A similar meeting of nature and art occurs near the kitchen terrace, where an open, square sculpture frames a formal, terrace-end planting of banked bergenia, from which emerges the whimsy of a Cocktail rose, brilliant red in early spring.

Floral color is used here only for accents, just as in the old *bastide* gardens, but with a view to visual play: a swath of orange gazanias spreading near the terracotta tiles of the kitchen terrace, for example.

Above the house, three small strips of terraced hillside can only be discovered by coming upon them directly at the top of narrow stairs: the lowest features a long basin. At its far end, olive trunks, framed by another

Bronze triangles and squares by Bruno Romeda echo and answer natural forms in this contemporary sculpture garden. Celebrated music critic Margaret Likierman compared its studied, formal complexities to those of the late Beethoven quartets.

*In a garden
r Valbonne, the
eway happily
nces the shapes and
rs of common
ts: oleander,
as, olive trees,
resses, and lavender
ow).*

square sculpture, are set off by the strong shapes of acanthus, cypress, and a cherry laurel hedge. Above, pittosporum encloses roses rambling on wires, and still higher up, a row of citrus trees stands against another dark hedge. Huge agaves discourage further exploration of storage areas beyond.

If instead of going straight up the hill one turns left, a small, narrowly hedged-in path suddenly emerges onto the swimming pool, itself enclosed by clipped greenery on three sides. The pool area has the best view of the property, left wide open . . . but framed by another well-placed bronze sculpture, a square named *Quadrata*.

A soft-toned, ocher-colored wall back at the western corner of the pool space contains an intriguing slit, like those of medieval battlements—only this one was designed by contemporary architect Jean-Michel Wilmotte, a family friend and sometimes resident. Looking through it, one can barely make out the modern studio behind. Presumably the opening is useful for communications between working artists and swimming families.

Going toward the front, west end of the pool terrace, one may happen upon a tiny, diamond-patterned santolina parterre, shaded by

a persimmon tree, which gives access to the studio buildings. In front of their French doors, two old olive trees and a pergola shade a patio full of pots, its square tiles repeating the design of the windowpanes. It is planted with fragrant pelargoniums and flowers in whites and blues. A niche in the stone wall at the far end contains fragments of Roman pottery, the lines of which are as modern as anything else in the garden.

So it is that the whole domain spreads out on all sides of the house, above and below. Discreet, almost hidden paths lead first to this, then to that dramatically framed feature. No single itinerary takes precedence, nor have any been planned for stately promenades. The lines of terracing have been exploited in countless original ways, the huge olive trees providing stability, form, mass, and muted color all at once. Whether the scenic elements are grown or constructed, they all work marvelously together at the artists' command.

SCULPTURE, OAKS, AND OLIVE TREES

Sculpture gardens, as a genre, are flourishing on the Riviera today, and certainly the above example must count among the most successful. Several new ones are in the making, too

*Old oaks
and olive trees are
treated as individual
sculptures, among
which are placed works
by artists like Andy
Goldsworthy. Free-
flowing bougainvillea
and lavender contrast
colorfully with dark
green frames of cypress
and ivy on the façade
(facing and above).*

Near
Valbonne, well-pruned
olive crowns back
ivy-coated pillars over
which cascades an
untamed, rambling red
rose. All of these
gardens use terracotta
urns to provide
warm notes and formal
accents (here with
a pittosporum globe).

young as yet for description. Generally their owners are artists or art collectors, for whom the shapes, volumes, spaces, colors, and textures of a garden simply extend the art of sculpture into nature itself. Often the result, as in the Courtright-Romeda garden, is witty as well as elegant. Another mature example belonging to gallery owners has been designed on three acres of low, spreading terraces beyond Valbonne. This open site lends itself beautifully to viewing plants as well as objects from all angles. The grounds support not only a hundred oil-producing olive trees but a grove of fifty-year-old deciduous oaks, whose spreading, dense, dark canopies and gnarled trunks also provide great character and sometimes serve to frame artwork. Near one group, a sculpture by Ben, perfectly imitating a Swiss road sign, proclaims "Switzerland does not exist." The owner explains that this is a favorite of her mother-in-law, who is Swiss.

One enters through a gate at the bottom of the property. Here the driveway has been enclosed by two formal bands of olive trees pruned into balls, interspersed with oleander, with strips of lavender at their feet—a simple planting which could be imitated in any Mediterranean garden. When this approach road suddenly opens onto the broad terraces with the house above, the effect is striking and pleasing.

The densest oak grove sits off to the left of the driveway. In its heart, a long rectangle of bare earth has been reserved for players of *boules*, the popular Mediterranean version of lawn bowls. A sculpture by J. Diffring presides on a pedestal at the near end, a head

called *L'Œil intérieur* which, in spite of its name, seems to observe the *boules* players with benevolence. Its smooth folds provide a favorite haven for the family cat.

The best sculpture of the entire garden is one enormous, spreading oak which gave the house its name (Le Mas du Roure) and probably dates from the Renaissance. The garden has been designed in such a way that this majestic tree serves as its major focal point, where the driveway ends in a circle.

Since the pool is also on the level above, it remains largely invisible. It is enclosed by a high, ivy-covered wall against which a formal line of coronilla stands out bright yellow in early spring, on the far side. On the bank below the pool, bands of rosemary, hebes, and cotoneasters separate it from the driveway. A mock ruined tower, ivy-smothered, rises at the west end and supports a diving platform above the pool.

As a pendant to the grand oak, an ancient olive tree rises on the other side of the paved circle, framing the house and the space immediately in front of it. Here the garden remains formal and geometrical, a repetition of squares and rectangles in different textures and sizes. The house façade is neatly and playfully transformed into patterned spaces on either side of the two tall cypress sentinels flanking the main door. To the east, a carefully contained rectangle of dark ivy has been trained around the windows, whereas, to the west, an exuberant, brilliant bougainvillea has been given free rein.

Directly in front of the main door, a sheltered patio repeats the same shapes: a large

square of paved path encloses a smaller square of emerald lawn, with a box dome at each of its four corners. Raised beds set against these east and west lines provide color through a succession of bulbs and annual flowers. Set here and there in the paving are shaved cubes of silvery santolina. Steps lead down to the rough grass beyond, with large terracotta pots at each end. The prospect is strikingly framed by a large bronze square—by Bruno Romeda. A bit further down the hill, a bronze triangle leads the eye still farther afield.

All around this bright but formal heart extend the gently graded terraces with wilder plantings. Olive trees punctuate the east side of the garden much as the oaks dominate the west side, separated by the curving driveway; but in fact there is no deliberate segregation of the two types of tree, similar in size and spreading shape, but so different in color and texture. Both are carefully pruned so that their trunks catch the strong southern light. Groves of shrubs, clipped into soft globes (terebinths, laurels), or grouped into spiky clumps (yuccas), set them off. In some places, where just the foundations of old stone walls have survived, these provide planter beds for small-scaled sedums or little aloes.

There is no single itinerary through this part of the garden, so that the stroller discovers a series of different, semi-natural tableaux among the trees. A number of other sculptures appear here and there, usually placed in a spot chosen by their creators. The owners are awaiting a new one by Andy Goldsworthy, whose witty transformations of natural, rustic materials into art would be particularly appropriate for their garden.

This agricultural property was first transformed into a garden for a former governor of the Bank of England. Today it mingles most harmoniously its rural setting, sculptural trees, floral décor, and contemporary art.

A SIMPLE, RUSTIC GARDEN

If some terraced hillsides of old *bastide* domains have thus evolved into sophisticated, self-aware gardens, settings for avantgarde art and art works in their own right, others maintain a mood of rustic simplicity, as earthy and at the same time as elegant as the rough-glazed local pottery.

One terraced domain near Grasse has survived largely unchanged for the last fifty years, a particularly unspoiled example of the Mediterranean country garden. A member of one of France's great gardening families created it just after World War II out of rural fragments—an old sheepfold now joined to a blacksmith's workshop forms a single, golden-toned house. The olive terraces, flanked by vineyards, extend on the slope below, and a neighborhood shepherd still uses the lower reaches for pasture.

The current owner's mother designed the garden herself. It has remained much as in her time, although the cityscape beyond the property limits has changed utterly. The approach road descending to the north side of the house makes lavish use of banked irises and wisteria against the rounded, evergreen shapes of laurel and boxwood. But the site's

In this rustic country domain, unchanged for the last fifty years, the family dines by the old well, under the magic tracery of interlocking plane trees. This garden is said to be haunted, but the spirits are clearly benevolent.

most compelling feature is the broad, raised, stone-paved terrace south of the house. Here were planted four plane trees which have been carefully pruned to provide a flat ceiling for this outdoor room. The lacework of their canopies has now spread so successfully that some of the branches have been grafted together, from tree to tree, to solidify the structure. A round, weathered stone trough lies in the center of this dining terrace, under the tracery of these branches, with table and chairs nearby.

From this raised platform, a double flight of steps leads downward to the terrace running along the south façade of the house, some two meters below. It shelters between its wings a simple half-moon pool and fountain.

On the lower level, a long rectangle of green lawn extends westward, the length of the house façade, closed at the far end by a semicircle of squared-off cypresses. Rising behind their green curtain, old olive trees are almost smothered by climbing white and yellow Banksia roses. In the early spring, they make a splendid show from the dining platform opposite. Raised beds running the length of the grassy rectangle on both sides present traditional planting mixtures: bergenia, nepeta, peonies, the outer edge punctuated by smooth green boxwood balls.

From this formal space, one looks directly down on the broad top of a wrought-iron pergola built on the level below. The roses it sports offer a sea of fragrant bloom right at the feet of strollers and diners.

The house façade rises along the northern side of the lawn rectangle. It helps support a second pergola made of old beams and rough, stone pillars, overrun by trumpets of pale blue morning-glory and indigo thunbergia. Among the broken paving slabs under this pergola grow self-sown purple spikes of *Verbena rigida*, the pink and white daisy flowers of vittidinia, and the orange tissue-paper petals of eschscholzia, often called California poppies.

Steps by the west corner of the house lead upward past a square landing, an expanse carpeted half with deep blue ceratostigma, half with golden gazanias. Still farther west, behind the cypress curtain which closes the perspective from the dining terrace, paths lead into wild woodland (covering about four acres), in the midst of which stands an old shrine to Notre Dame.

On the garden's lower terraces, the first levels have kept a garden character, each with a different mood. One has yet another pergola, covered with roses and backed by a dense, squared-off cypress hedge. A box circle with more roses, and stone edging, sports

groups of *Salvia involucrata*. Farther below, multitrunked Judas trees are crowned with deep cerise flowers before the leaves emerge in March. Many mature trees, formal designs, and self-sown flowers combine to create an atmosphere of great charm and ease.

The owner of this garden spent many years as an ethnologist in Africa. She seems to experience nature with an extra sense, a special depth, which encompasses the century-old trees, the woodland shrine, and even the electric company's mammoth pylons at her gate as one mystic whole. Are there really phantom horses coursing through the patio from time to time? In the magic seclusion of this timeless garden, their presence is entirely believable.

TWO COUNTRY NEIGHBORS

Two beautiful properties east of Grasse have also preserved an atmosphere of comfortable, rustic simplicity. At the same time, however, they exemplify strikingly different treatments of the classic, terraced hillside—that of the landscaper, and that of the plant enthusiast. The first is the work of celebrated designer Jean Mus, who, with the help of his eager clients, established the garden in just two years. The second was elaborated by plant collectors who made the garden part by part, as they found time to expand, over a forty-year period. This couple has only just retired to a city apartment, for health reasons, and sold the property to young people who are keen to learn about the garden and maintain it, with the help of its creators. Thus both domains belong today to active professional people, who in both cases have taken on a garden largely created by someone else.

Each property is hidden from the outside world by the hillside rising behind, and by thick plantings along an upper wall. For both, a discreet but elegant gate opens from the west onto a long, planted driveway which leads to a salmony-pink *bastide* with pale turquoise shutters. Both give onto the wide valley with its Tuscan-like view of rolling, cypress-planted hills. Both are breathtaking from the moment of arrival, and both reserve many surprises for the visitor who takes the time to meander from terrace to terrace, downhill and back up again.

The Mus garden, called La Ferme Saint-Jean, lies around a seventeenth-century farmstead which once belonged to the Villa Croisset, an estate designed by Ferdinand Bac, now demolished. Jean Mus's father was head gardener at the Villa Croisset, and Mus remembers playing barefoot on this land as a boy. He has treated the garden with true affection,

At the Ferme Saint-Jean, t... driveway is edged with a delicate patte... of box, agapanthus, ceratostigma aroun... citrus globes, all und... high olive canopies. It ends in a stand of cypresses with shiny circles of ligul... at their feet.

and a keen appreciation for its site, its light, its special tones, and its nuances of color.

This farmstead remained agricultural until after World War II when it was renovated for movie star Martine Carroll, whose main legacy to the present garden is a stand of palm trees by the swimming pool below. On the dry slope above the driveway, a more recent owner tried rhododendrons, and grew ivy up the trunks of all the olive trees (which he found ugly). This area has been cleared, and the spreading olive trunks now emerge from drifts of silvery helichrysum, bergenia, and flowing, flat, groundcover junipers.

Mus has chosen to stress the country character of the garden. The olive terracing provides its main theme, even as regards color: Mus feels that in Provence, to the west, the mistral wind imposes brilliant light and bright blue skies, whereas here, in the Riviera backcountry, sky and olive foliage blend into a softer, subtle, and harmonious whole. So it is that these trees' imposing silver crowns dominate the garden. At the same time, Mus has preserved the ancient specimens which best frame the views opposite—sky, mountain, and distant sea. Enhanced by cypresses and two new lime canopies right in front of the house itself, these plantings provide a series of windows onto the valley opposite.

The original dirt driveway has been paved with Italian tiles alternating with well-proportioned grass strips, to emphasize its length. Mus always pays much attention to the textures which carpet a garden, whether plant or mineral, flat or organized into a pattern of different heights. At the foot of the retaining wall which extends along the driveway's upper side, small lemon trees alternate in a recurrent pattern with santolina clumps, low box balls, daubs of ceratostigma, and agapanthus—a kind of long tapestry strip. It culminates in a huge stand of *Ligularia tussilaginea*, whose fat, shiny leaves spread at the foot of an old stone fountain trickling peacefully in the summer air. Three very smooth cypress towers of different girths stand guard by the fountain and mark the juncture of path and house.

The olive trees on each side of the road are kept pruned to the same height, although those on the left grow out of a terrace one level above. This is the sort of subtle touch

of invention which makes the general design all hang together so well.

A pebbled path winds downward through the olive trees to the swimming pool, which is invisible from above. The passage resembles the old donkey tracks of hillside farms. Its rough, stone surface around a central canal ensures safe walking and good drainage—and provides another strong design. Jean Mus uses whenever possible these traditional solutions to practical problems which also involve country materials, usually beautiful in themselves and in the patterns they make. The old olive plantations continue below the driveway, their terracing emphasized first by open lawn, then by low hedging and groundcover planting—a wonderful stretch of carefully trained Mermaid roses.

The house and its terrace stand at the hub of a half-wheel of perspectives west, south, and east. The driveway arrives from the west, the donkey path leads down the hill to the rambling hedges southwest. Directly in front, beyond the new limes of the house patio, the tops of the palm trees hint at the swimming pool on the level below.

The area rising east of the house provides a whole catalogue of planting possibilities for small-scaled terraces. Some are bisected by stone steps leading downhill, with blocks of lavender close to the house providing foreground plantings for tall trees at the far end. Other terraces are allowed to glory in their very length. The long driveway arriving from the west has as its eastern counterpart an extended, wrought-iron pergola planted with Banksia roses and jasmines. Citrus bushes alternate with terracotta pots along the back edge. At the farthest point, a very sheltered little bench under an ivy roof is enclosed by sculpted laurustinus. This enclosed, protected spot contrasts with the openings onto the valley offered between climbing plants along the way. On all of these levels, old olive trees punctuate, shelter, provide structure and solidity. They are never lost in the design, but instead anchor it.

Below the pergola, more patterned tapestry strips also stress the horizontals: a row of citrus is underplanted with alternating arum lilies and the blue spikes of perovskia or Russian sage, with daisy-flowered *Eriocephalus* spilling over the outer edges. Still

A talented local mason has redone the terrace walls at the Ferme Saint-Jean so that they look as if they had always been there. They are underplanted here with Convolvulus cneorum *and* Polygonum capitatum *(center).*

Beautiful details include the harmony of simplici and sophistication at this fountain, set a froth of daisy-like vittidinia (facing pa

further below, a row of young olive trees is more simply planted in a carpet of creeping thyme, with dwarf pittosporum globes at their feet.

At the bottom of this eastern series of terraces, clearly visible from the house patio but situated well below it, is a long, narrow, rectangular basin. Outlined in lawn and enclosed by box domes at each corner, it creates a compelling focal point in the middle distance. A broad flight of stone steps descends toward the basin from the house, enclosed by low, billowing, rockery plantations—particularly the creeping *Polygonum capitatum* which has vivid pink-purple flowers and deep red foliage in fall. Mingled with vittidinia, lilies, silver convolvulus, and dwarf evergreens, this curving, spilling descent creates an island of informality at the very heart of this highly structured composition.

The tapestried terrace strips thus rise in tiers above this rockery and the formal basin lies beyond. Immediately below, several narrow levels have been simply planted with lawn and edged with stone, to bring out their strong lines and rhythms. Further down the hill extends a whole hillside of ancient olive trees, sheltering here a vegetable garden, there fruit trees and vines, elsewhere kept in rough grass mowed with respect for the seasonal carpets of anemones, wild orchids, and daisies which characterize all these sites.

How similar and how different is the garden at the nearby property of Fort de France. The site, the view, the architecture, the respect for country traditions are much

the same. Here too, the gate gives no idea of the rich garden behind, but the long driveway, also arriving from the west, is densely lined with plants. In this garden, they do not form a pattern whose rhythms lead one onward toward the house, but an array so compelling that one simply must stop and take it in bit by bit. Every detail demands attention, even as a red-flowered bignonia calls from the façade at the far end. There is nothing haphazard about the arrangement, however: colors, volumes, and shapes of both flowers and foliage have been artfully blended, punctuated by half-sunken earthenware pots full of helianthemums, centaureas, pelargoniums of various kinds and colors, and the delightful tiny green balloons of *Cardiospermum*. Climbing roses spread their fans along the back wall, but the tall, dark blue-flowering sage *Salvia guaranitica* has also been espaliered to excellent effect, like a climber. Other sages mingle with citrus, different solanums, several colors of bell-shaped abutilons including the variety with variegated foliage, a rare clump of *Fabiana* 'Violacea', and real exotics like banana trees. Halfway along stands an intricate, multi-layered topiary created from an unusual *Pittosporum heterophyllum*.

As the path reaches the house, steps to the left, edged with a wealth of pots, lead upward to terraces above the driveway. On the main one, an open space for playing children or dining parents has been arranged under spreading planes, whose umbrella spokes have again been grafted together to

At Fort de France, the informal driveway is lined with richly colored and scented treasures in great variety, catching the eye and the nose at every step.

Where such perfumed profus could overwhelm design, olive jars—h half-buried among aloes and Beloperone guttata—provide punctuation and soli (facing page).

create a ceiling. Further along one moves among interesting groups of larger shrubs and trees—a rare and elegant metasequoia with two separate, spreading trunks; a tree ceanothus beautifully planted next to the yellow-flowering ornamental cherry 'Yukon' and the pale mauve-flowered *Buddleja officinalis*, all three blooming together in April.

It is impossible to convey the wealth of secret corners in this garden and all the treasures they contain. Sometimes an ordinary plant, a common cistus, becomes striking because it was allowed to grow woody, its stems pruned to show off its twisting shapes and warm tones. All over, an endless variety of small-scaled groundcovers and rockery plants create different textures: *Alchemilla mollis* and red-leaved ajugas, a pale pink-flowered mesembryanthemum, a deep pink polygonum around small iris. Low hedges of santolina, box, and euonymus impose a semblance of order.

Silvery Helichrysum petiolare *(perennial on the Riviera) threads its way through the upright stems of* Euphorbia characias *in a delightful contrast of tones and textures beneath the blue shutters of the villa at Fort de France.*

Shady passages behind the house lead to several different gardens on the east terraces: shaded woodland at the top, including such surprises as the exceptional *Bauhinia* ("mountain ebony" or "orchid tree"); a rose garden outlined in santolina hedging, packed with other shrubs, lilies, and perennials for all seasons such as pink creeping jasmine, *Hydrangea arborescens* 'Anabelle' with its flat-topped umbels, lobelias, a huge tuft of sword-leaved orchid *Bletilla striata*; the whole backed by twin yew trees; a rock garden around an autumn-flowering cherry, where foxgloves sow themselves (unusual in this region), and where a creeping, white-starred saxifrage replaces lawn. There are roses throughout, not only in a separate garden; a good many are the old varieties created by Nabonnand, including 'Général Schablikine', a kind of heritage rose on the Côte d'Azur, already admired by Lord Brougham when he gardened in Cannes.

Below the house extend several terraces of vegetable plantings, most decoratively maintained by the original owners but too demanding, at the moment, for the new family which has just taken over the property. Further downhill, remnants of the old olive terraces now seem dull in contrast to the profusion above. The would-be explorer is not in fact invited to descend; steps upward lead back to the house terrace with its shady canopy of paulownia leaves.

This enchanting domain has taken forty years to mature. Indeed, its garden heritage is much older than that, for this is the very property described by Lady Fortescue, her first southern garden, in *Perfume from Provence*.

The Ferme Saint-Jean, a designer's creation, and the Fort de France, a plantsman's paradise, sit on the same hillside only a few kilometers apart. It is perhaps unfair to compare a mature garden with one which is just being created. Yet one can already appreciate the different, but equally compelling, attractions of two totally different approaches to gardening. In the property which Jean Mus has created for his clients, the main lines of the garden are easily readable already from the entranceway, all the more so from the house terrace, with only the swimming pool hidden away. These perspectives have been carefully weighed for their pleasurable proportions, just as the view has not been taken for granted but deliberately framed. None of which precludes surprises and invitations to further exploration; but the plantings serve to lead one onward, and bring out the general design. Texture counts here too, in both foliage and mineral elements. But the landscaper uses plants in swaths, whereas at Fort de France, rarely does one find two samples of the same variety together. In the latter garden, where a triangle of lagerstreomias graces an upper corner, they turn out to have three different colors of bloom. Mus surely would have planted three of the same hue.

In the designer garden, the house is anchored to its setting by the traditional climbers and pots, but it is clearly the hub of the wheel. In the collectors' garden, the house at its center is not a focal point but one more support for plants, which lean against and around it like vines on a trellis.

Some will revel in the abundance of the collections at Fort de France, others may find them cluttered and claustrophobic. A lover of garden architecture will appreciate the elegance of the Mus garden, while a plant collector might find it poorly furnished.

In fact, both gardens offer a profusion of plants: a swath of Mermaid roses used as groundcover conveys just as great a sense of exuberance as does a densely mixed planting —and certainly a greater feeling of motion. The collectors' garden is more static; one moves through it very slowly. Both have a wonderful, old-fashioned atmosphere, and both, even the recent creation, bear the mark of long years of love for the site. Mus has been faithful to his boyhood memories.

JEAN MUS "CHEZ LUI"

Unlike other internationally-known designers who work on the Riviera, Jean Mus comes from a local family, which arrived from Italy in 1650. Moreover, his father's experience as a practical gardener was not lost on the son, giving him a sense of plants which many landscape architects lack.

Jean Mus works at Cabris, east of Grasse. His own garden is a deeply personal conception. It occupies about an acre, and has now ripened for some twenty-five years.

Starting from his beloved terraces of olive trees, Mus has created a series of itineraries which move from enclosure to enclosure, each framing anew the space beyond— and behind. This is a garden with no straight lines. And it is above all a foliage garden, full of subtle color contrasts; there is never the crude shock of red leaves among green but always gentle gradation and carefully studied nuance. There are flowers too, but they mainly serve to mark the varieties of seasonal change. Part of this garden's strength is its year-round appeal.

Along the road, a high wall protects the property from outside curiosity. Just inside the gate, a lower wall is topped by a geometrical arrangement of dwarf pittosporum and silver-leaved, shrubby convolvulus. Here one can turn left (east), or right (west). The latter option leads toward the house entrance, where a patio displays unusual pot plantings: a low terracotta jar mingles small-scaled bamboo with ivy and a dwarf pittosporum in an interesting contrast of shapes and colors; a taller one uses a simple mix of oleander with vittidinia spilling over its edge; or an orange tree pruned low, with small-leaved, creeping hebe and a touch of red foliage at its feet.

Behind the house, an intriguing geometrical arrangement of aromatic plants extends on two levels—thyme, mint, savory, and *Lavandula stoechas* are flanked by silver convolvulus, dwarf pittosporum, and cistus with small, pink flowers. These perfume the passage to an open sheepfold, converted into another picturesque patio area. A sheltered wooden sundeck lies to the west, from which a small path winds through the trees down the hillside. From this top level, looking southwest, the entire valley leading toward Draguignan unfolds in a spectacular succession of hilltops. The lower part of the garden is, however, self-contained and turned inward.

The main descent leads east from the entrance gate. The path is enclosed by banks of cistus, nandinas, and pink-flowering rosemary (the one whose creation is attributed to the vicomte de Noailles), underplanted again with that wonderful, non-stop flowering, self-sowing plant, vittidinia (*Erigeron karvinskianus*). The path winds downhill, past a magnificent patch of golden "Burmese" day lilies, past a multi-trunked Judas tree at a junction, then through a laurel arch toward the pool. But its destination remains mysterious. The spaces remain hidden from each other until one arrives at a central crossroads, just above the pool. Here a red-leaved smoke bush (*Cotinus coggygria*) makes a dramatic focal point.

One can go either east or west at this point, along or downward, but the destinations are again blocked from immediate view, here by a sentinel pillar of variegated *Pittosporum tenuifolium*, flanked by two kinds of bamboo (broad and fine-leaved), the shrubby China rose *odorata* 'Sanguinea', the whole grouping underplanted with hardy fuchsias. This mixture is typical of the happy blending of rust, yellow, and gray tones in this garden.

The longest perspective in this complex domain lies east of the pool, where two olive tree terraces, separated by a height of about 5 feet (1.5 meters) at the start, merge at the far end. One can thus easily enter on one level and circle back on the other.

Their juncture with the path descending from above is navigated thanks to a short flight of stone steps, set among a small rockery. A whole spectrum of small-leaved groundcover spills over the walls here: a fascinating, small-scaled garden, which includes complete in a few square meters creeping rosemaries, silver convolvulus, and one of Mus's favorite

In the private garden of designer Jean Mus, these few steps linking two terraces of olive trees are set off by low, spreading pittosporums, vittidinia, and polygonum. Russian sage (Perovskia) and creeping rosemary complete the picture.

groundcovers, the low-growing *Polygonum capitatum* with reddish-green foliage, which makes deep pink carpets when it flowers. Visible in the same glance is the red cotinus along the path uphill, and swaths of vittidinia mixed with brilliant silver and blue perovskia on the level above. There is an effect of foreshortening, layer upon layer, again a kind of plant tapestry rich in tone and texture.

On the uppermost of the two olive tree terraces spreading east of this junction, three grand old specimens have become the center of low plantations—not islands but peninsulas, which thrust out from the long line of the back retaining wall. These low, banked curves, backed by nandinas, laurel, pittosporum, oleander, honeysuckle, cistus, and

bare rock and the same creeping polygonum.

On the next level down, below this central, two-tiered composition, a wilder path, dense with artemisias, ivy, and loosely trimmed box, leads back below the pool. Suddenly, in a secret corner, the level changes slightly, and one discovers a small square patch, a mosaic of low shrubs in contrasting tones and shapes, a jewel of a garden in miniature. The pool itself, blocked at its east end by the poolhouse, seems to turn its back on the two olive terraces. It has a world of its own, a slightly exotic one, thanks to a mixed planting at its west end centered on tall palm trees with red and yellow tones, a clump of olives, a sculptural *Mahonia lomariifolia* and a broad block of variegated *Pit-*

much more, set off the trunks and provide a flowing rhythm to the otherwise straight grassy path which goes past them on the outside edge of the terrace, which in turn is bordered with creeping Corsican rosemary.

The lower level has a box hedge on the outside, punctuated with terracotta jars at regular intervals. Their effect is to enclose these two olive terraces as a separate, mainly grassy garden area, the largest of the property.

A particularly ornamental, twin-trunked olive tree presides over the distant point where the two terraces merge. In the evenings, its sculptural forms are lit by a lamp (cunningly hidden behind two terracotta roof tiles) which shines upward into the branches with a beautiful effect of chiaroscuro. This majestic tree is set among

tosporum tenuifolium. Dwarf fan palms flank tall laurels supporting Banksia roses, with another 'Sanguinea' rose, which Mus loves, at their feet. A single, tall cypress marks the convergence of lines at the back retaining wall, ideally set against a curving hillside in the distance.

Along the pool's north side, the retaining wall has been planted with densely spilling shapes of pittosporum and rosemary, mingled with brilliant daubs of lantanas, dwarf pomegranates and fuchsias—one of the spots of brightest color in the garden. Above it extends another open terrace carpeted with lawn, where more olive trees shade a stone table and benches. The focal point at the terrace's west end is an old stone well. It is backed by a striking but simple association of shrubby horse chestnut (*Aesculus parviflora*) with its thicket growth and large leaves, set in an island of creeping ceratostigma, rich with deep blue flowers in late summer, and wonderful red foliage for a long time in the fall.

This is not a creation for those who shun reds and yellows in their gardens—or rather, it is just the place to convince the doubting how marvelous these colors can be when used with taste and tact. Golden day lilies, clumps of fuchsias, blue and red ceratostigma, pink and red polygonum, multicolored but soft-toned vittidinia, silver-leaved artemisias, helichrysums, and convolvulus are favorite underplantings throughout.

Much attention has been paid to the textures of foliage as well as to their colors. Mus

differences of level, color, and texture pay homage to the kings of the garden, the ancient olive trees.

A PHOTOGRAPHER'S GARDEN

Naturally enough, Mus often has occasion to landscape similar sites. Whether more steep or less, each presents different problems and new solutions. A garden belonging to a professional garden photographer in the modern village of Castellane has a completely different feel—much more open onto the landscape on all sides. Mountains rise dramatically to the north, sea views spread to the south. From the road, the property slopes downward to the house, which separates the gar-

Jean Mus skillfully alternates sheltered corners with vast perspectives, as here above his own swimming pool. The olive tree remains for him a cherished symbol of Mediterranean light and life.

believes in repeating the same basic leaf shape within a group of shrubs, but with variants. A garden, he feels, should have a kind of discretion in its effects: a jasmine may be hidden behind other plants, draping a wall, so that its presence is mainly felt because of its fragrance, even when its exact location cannot be easily discovered. Behind the swimming pool, for example, in a small corner that would not normally be noticed, a lagerstroemia, a kumquat, and a fig tree surround the pool shower, providing privacy and occasional refreshing delicacies for swimmers.

This garden also plays very much on open and closed spaces. The mountain opposite provides yet another curved, enclosing line high on the horizon, giving a sense of shelter to the lower reaches. But all of the site's

den into two parts: the approach path winding among olive trees and grassy strips above, and the pool area, semi-paved, more formal and exotic, below. All around the house, trellises protect small patios paved with soft-toned terracotta tiles which link garden and living spaces. Kumquats are a favorite accent plant here, their orange fruit picking up on the terracotta warmth against dark, evergreen foliage, often flanked by tumbling, bright blue-flowered Corsican rosemaries and the paler, sky-blue felicia.

From the entrance gate, the house is invisible. In most places here, the original stone retaining walls have been removed and in this instance they have been replaced by gentle grading on both sides of a winding, flagstone path. This does not obliterate the

*In this
mountain garden, the
original terracing
has been largely
replaced by grassy
banks. Stone walls now
mark transitions
and support accent
plantings like these
osteospermum, spilling
under olive trees pruned
into high crowns.*

levels but softens the transitions, an unusual treatment of such a hillside and one which required careful technical planning, so that heavy seasonal rains do not remove all the topsoil. Mus has managed here to preserve the feeling of gradual unfolding, each level revealing a new vista, while at the same time creating a visual sense of flow.

An evenly spaced row of cypresses protects the left side of the scene at the entrance. Already, a dozen venerable olive trees emerge from beds and drifts of typically Mediterranean plants: myrtle, eleagnus, cistus, upright rosemary, shrub roses, underplanted with pale blue-flowering felicia, agapanthus clumps, eriocephalus, silver convolvulus, and the aster-like *Felicia filifolia*. In each case, a group of tall shrubs is underplanted with irregularly spilling groundcovers, from which the olive tree trunks rise up as the central feature of the composition. Jean Mus has developed a pruning method for olive trees aimed at ornamental display rather than production, which creates soaring lines and crowns here silhouetted against the far-off mountains.

As the main entrance path descends, the house first becomes visible as a line of weathered, orange roof tiles, partially draped by a white-starred *Clematis armandii*, splendid in March. Soon after, one comes on one of the property's most original features: a semicircular flight of low steps, with box balls on either side, leading down to the house entrance. In front of the door is an elegantly paved circle, a mosaic of stone and pebbles. Massed by the descent, cascading plants are

lower, the texture finer, to bring out the design: felicias, creeping rosemaries, small-leaved cistus like 'Peggy Sammons', heavily pruned *Teucrium fruticans* and especially lavenders, including the winter flowering species, *dentata*. Spreading olive crowns lean over the entrance from the sides, providing shade, giving support to the climbing roses which frame the door, and completing the circular pattern in the air.

Protected paths and steps lead downward on both sides of the house, connecting the series of small patios with the pool area beyond. The lower side of the house gives onto a vast panorama of both mountains and sea. The swimming pool lies in the foreground, half-encircled by the building itself. Its discreet rectangle is set off by the striking forms of loquats, yuccas, dwarf fan-palms, and more clumps of kumquat bushes. A border linking a particularly sculptural olive tree to the pool mingles feathery nandinas (sometimes called heavenly bamboo) with Corsican rosemary, with the velvety silver foliage of *Senecio greyi*, a massive sparmannia, creeping lantana, and plumbago.

Much of this area is paved with the same warm terracotta squares found on the side patios. Small differences of level and irregular angles increase the pleasurable sense of enclosure on one side, in contrast with the broad panorama opposite. House and garden here overlap thanks to the vaulted dining retreat built into the house, further shaded by a pergola, and the balcony on the level above, edged with dwarf pittosporum balls. Fragrant star jasmine climbs the house walls,

In a garden east of Grasse, an astrolabe stands on the lower terraces, flanked by two peach trees. Behind is the olive foliage which English gardeners in the south often plant near these trees.

its fulgent, dark green foliage setting off their soft ocher wash. Similarly, the tiny disks of muehlenbeckia make a green line against the risers of the terracotta steps.

On the lowest level of the garden, below the pool, another grassy sward leads off once more to secret places among shrubs and trees, which are more exotic and more densely packed this time, including eucalyptus and several varieties of mimosa. A ceanothus provides a striking accent, a pergola covered in jasmine provides scent and shade. Bay laurels constitute the basic hedge which protects the garden from the road curving below.

This, then, is the bottom of the garden, the end of an itinerary which starts with the entrance gate at its highest point. The presence of old olive trees throughout unifies all the variously planted parts. The strongly architectural character of stone retaining walls has been modified into serpentine slopes, but the feel of the garden still echoes the classic rural descent among majestic olive trees, and provides a dynamic unfolding of the site's possibilities.

TERRACED PLANT COLLECTIONS

The classic hillside olive orchard offers infinite design possibilities. At the same time, these plantations provide wonderfully protected spaces for rare plants. The high walls and sheltering tree canopies of such sites create special microclimates—put to good use for centuries by the perfume industry at Grasse. On such a slope, tender treasures can also be displayed in tiers without shading

each other. On occasion, the imposing lines of the architecture become obscured, and the powerful aesthetic appeal of the original setting overwhelmed by the profusion of individual specimens. But obviously different owners seek different pleasures.

An English couple gardening on a hillside east of Grasse has created a wealth of flower color from spring to fall, an exuberance much inspired by the "mixed border" model of their homeland. Many of their plants come, indeed, from England; but the bright and glad garden which they have created owes much to Mediterranean sunshine.

The garden's best feature, perhaps, is the two-levelled May border extending east of the pool. The outside edge of the upper terrace, marked by a rosemary hedge, also supports a striking row of Judas trees, rootsprouts trimmed onto a low trellis, much like vines. Farther along, a 'Seagull' rose spills over the wall and simultaneously climbs a long iron pergola, with great tufts of arum lilies at its foot.

A large olive tree in the middle of this border provides light shade and protection for a grand variety of plants: mixed iris, penstemons, phlomis and dianthus, English and old roses ('William Shakespeare', or softly scented 'Cornelia'), peonies, alstroemeria (the 'Ligtu' hybrids), and colorful shrubs such as the photinia 'Red Robin' with its bright red spring foliage, or a gold-leaved Mexican orange (*Choisya*), and variegated *wulfenii* spurge.

A whole hillside extends below, its original olive trees intermingled with a wide range of shrubs and trees, many Riviera specialties such as echiums, or the rarer *Dombeya* and

These owners love glad and gay colors: reds, pinks, and yellows against the duller greens of olive and cypress trees (following pages).

Solandra. On one outside terrace edge, amidst a broad swath of iris and day lilies, a multi-trunked sumac raises its velvety red spikes. In late summer, the violet flowers of a nearby snail tree (*Vitex agnus castus*) provide a lovely complement.

Further down, in an open space, an astrolabe has been mounted on a pedestal and surrounded by a circle of plants in contrasting-colored wedges (frankenia, white thyme, and yellow potentilla). On either side, a simple peach tree of the red-fleshed, rustic, sanguine variety provides height.

At the property's lowest limit, where there is abundant water, a small Japanese-inspired pool garden has been arranged, complete with bridge. A *boules* terrace sits nearby among mixed shrub borders, again well-stocked with rare specimens, usually one of each. The owner, who makes his own garden furniture, has designed an elaborate, neo-Gothic bench as the center of this composition. In a few years, this level should be well-shaded by a whole series of tall trees: paulownia, catalpa, liquidambar, ginko, tulip tree, and several maples.

Color here is deliberately bright so that it can also be enjoyed by an invalid parent from the house: one olive tree supports a 'Paul's Scarlet Climber' rose through its silver crown. An original pool house has been made out of an old gypsy wagon (or *roulotte*), its travels now over, a new life begun with fresh turquoise paint and gold trim. Annuals sown in March add extra color in the rough grass of some terraces: Shirley and California poppies mixed with blue cornflowers.

Terracing here means enjoyable views from above and below, but many itineraries are possible, no single one has been planned for dramatic unveilings or long perspectives. The owners treasure their olive trees, but find the enormous job of their upkeep, particularly the long, complicated pruning, somewhat overwhelming. Thus these old inhabitants remain a discreet and somewhat cluttered backdrop for a wealth of new acquisitions. Like all passionate collectors, the owners avidly seek out the rare bird, the new discovery. At the same time, they are trying hard to marry English style with Mediterranean resources, while ensuring color in all parts of the garden throughout the year.

Another English gardener prides herself on Japanese maples, arranging their brilliant autumn foliage to create unusual contrasts with the ubiquitous olive tree and exotic agaves.

Another English gardener, a collector of international reputation, has transformed his property into a showcase for rare plants—it even features an arboretum. This gentleman's trees and shrubs, set out in tiers on a hillside east of Grasse, draw knowledgeable visitors from all over the world. Yet this is a welcoming, homey garden, where a brilliant rockery at the entrance mingles old favorites and rarer finds: thymes, Corsican rosemary, peonies, agapanthus, different abutilons (yellow and purple), daisy-flowered dimorphothecas, warm-hued gazanias, lime-green euphorbias, and a mix of day lilies. The house sits comfortably back from its open patio, and in the lawn opposite stand two groups of old olive trees underplanted with squares of ceratostigma, fuchsias, and creeping hypericum.

From the house terrace, one can view an Italianate perspective down the hill, stone steps flanked by low rosemary hedges, descending to a stately jar. But the hedging allows access on both sides to the collections, which include specimens of several thousand different flowering plants. Among them, to cite only a few, are the very rare *Dais cotinifolia* with mauve fruit, tree dahlias, *Dombeya burgessiae*, broad-leaved *Senecio grandifolius*, and of course every imaginable datura and abutilon. Often this plant collector has sought out rare cultivars of well-known families: several unusual robinias and gleditsias, Judas trees, viburnums, pittosporums, *Lavatera* 'Eve Price', a *Ceanothus thyrsiflorus repens* 'Ken Taylor', or a *Hibiscus mutabilis* whose flowers change color from pink to white. Or, simply, shrubs which more people could grow if they were better known: fremontodendron; *Eupatorium ligustrinum* (otherwise known as *Ageratina ligustrina*) which flowers twice a year; the wonderfully fragrant tree broom, *Cytisus battandieri*; pink-flowered phlomis, or *Xanthoceras sorbifolium*. Some are so unusual that their exact naming is problematic: the owner and his fellow experts cannot decide if a particular Persian lilac is 'lacinata' or 'Afghanica'. The collection also includes a number of large trees, melias, cedars, and a *Cryptomeria japonica*. But the feel of the garden remains small-scaled, familiar, accessible, never monumental or showy. There is just enough room between specimens to move comfortably—and to discover close to the ground a range of rare bulbs. Such gardens present the Riviera kaleidoscope in yet another version, mixing and matching not period gardens or exotic styles but plant varieties.

Another English owner who gardens even higher up in the backcountry is particularly proud of her Japanese maples, which do grow very well under her spreading olive tree canopies and inflame the garden with their red brilliance. At the same time, her terraced hillside mingles old roses particularly characteristic of Riviera gardens (*hugonis, laevigata*, 'Général Schablikine', 'Complicata', the white 'Mortola'), peonies, winter-flowering buddlejas, irises of every hue, shrubby sophoras. Bitten like the others with the collector's bug, this owner considers that by experimenting ceaselessly with what will and will not work, she "spends her entire life playing chess in the garden." As a result, on the lower terraces, the original, majestic olive trees have all but disappeared amidst the mix of shrubs and small trees.

So it is that these terraces in the sun, so characteristic of the French Riviera, provide great advantages to gardeners of all persuasions. Collectors put to good use their stone retaining walls and the spreading canopies of their ancient orchards, while designers rise to the challenge of their imposing architecture. Certainly the forceful rhythms created by the walls themselves cannot be ignored with impunity. They can easily dominate those gardens which remain too tentative, or, on the contrary, become blurred by spottily-massed assemblages. The points where the walls meet and cross need special attention, as do ends of terraces, and the transitions from one to another—as Lawrence Johnston and the vicomte de Noailles understood so well. Sometimes the long horizontals are enhanced by the plantings, lending themselves to the elaboration of "walks," with or without pergolas. Sometimes they are cut into blocks, or dramatically opposed to vertical descents (pergolas can also run up and down the hillside). Their outlines must be visible from above and below as well as on a level; from afar, as well as close up. And if the gardens' backcountry

locations often provide more summer coolness than can be found in seaside gardens (Tobias Smollett, the eighteenth-century novelist, already thought it would be ideal to live on the coast in winter and near Grasse in the summer), their microclimates need careful managing.

The most spectacular terraced gardens are of course those which enhance the given architecture with rich plant texture and appropriate tones, combining the best of both the designer's and plantsman's worlds. Russell Page reflected deeply on these problems, taking the silvery reflections of the olive trees as a theme. Among the plants which he found compatible and complementary were lavenders, flag iris of all kinds, garden pinks, santolina, diplopappus, *Felicia amelloides*, *Aster pappei*, *Phlomis fruticosa*, various salvia species, and *Leonotis leonurus* to "make a flowery groundwork." For "a bolder and greener look, bay laurels, *Choisya ternata*, the lovely late-flowering *Lagerstroemia indica*, agapanthus and tree peonies will compose another kind of picture, always in the same basic frame of olive trees." All these plants are readily available in specialized Riviera nurseries today. From the rural, Provençal *bastides* with comfortable but formal designs; to contemporary sculpture gardens which play on perspectives and geometries and consider ancient trees themselves as artworks; to a renewal with the rustic simplicity of country gardens; to contemporary landscaping, formal and informal; and, finally, to the treasure troves of plant collectors, the range is great. One basic site contains all of these possibilities, and of course many more can also be found. If one starts, however, not from a given topography but from a particular garden style, one can also discover an astonishing variety of original creations. Intimate gardens, a genre largely ignored by Riviera observers and one which is fast evolving, exist not only on the smaller-scaled terraced hillsides but in every conceivable setting. Private and personal by definition, and increasingly popular, they add a wealth of new interest to the French Riviera kaleidoscope.

Admirers
d-leaved plants set
ng Mediterranean
s often choose
urple smoke bush
nus coggygria)
he simple, green
ty also possesses
nt foliage, fall
, and plumy
rs (center).

The bright
blue balls of creeping
ceanothus tumble
over walls in many
smaller Riviera gardens
(following pages).

INTIMATE GARDENS

Intimate gardens have existed on the Riviera since at least the 1920s—secluded havens for family and friends, without vast perspectives or spectacular effects. Indeed, they are sometimes put together in a rather piecemeal manner, with a cosy and cottagey feel. In contrast, old Provençal and *bastide* gardens, while also country, family retreats, were at the same time large agricultural properties with formal outlines and parterres, and majestic, light-filtering trees. Flowers counted mainly as seasonal accents set against the clipped greenery. Intimate gardens today, especially on the Riviera where so many subtropical plants have been acclimatized, are usually small and brilliantly ornamental. They owe more to the English horticultural movement than to regional roots.

Mrs. Martineau's famous book about Riviera properties in the 1920s, *Gardening in Sunny Lands*, illustrates the fashion for floral abundance which was then becoming predominant. Describing the Villa Rosemary of Cap Ferrat, she makes no mention of architect Harold Peto's grand, Italianate design. Rather she praises rapturously its "southern riot of colour wisely and skilfully restrained." She deems the Villa Garibondy farther down the coast "one of the most Romantic gardens of the Riviera," not for Queen Victoria's monumental parasol pine but for a hilltop overgrown with wilder pines and tall cypresses, where "a riot of flowers are left to grow as they like. . . silver-leaved lupins with blue flowers seed themselves everywhere, mingling with patches of narcissus and *Iris stylosa*. Exochorda flings its white blossoms above a bank of anemones, and a big plumy bush of ephedra streams over all like a nereid's hair." She much prefers, "in contrast to the formal style" of many gardens, the "homelike" villa of Lady Foress at Menton.

The quintessentially English word "home-like" aptly describes the intimate style. Such gardens are generally made by the owners themselves for the enjoyment of their immediate circle—and by owners with a passion for plants. This blend of personal involvement and plantsmanship is also deemed typically English by garden historians, at least English ones, who claim that continental garden owners left the care of their properties to professionals and servants until the present century. It is true that Lawrence Johnston amazed visitors at la Serre de la Madone by greeting them in his gardening trousers, with dirt on his hands. But whatever the national influences may have been, the fashion for intimate gardening certainly owes much to the declining availability of cheap labor. This in turn was a factor in the development of the new, horticultural trend to which Johnston so much contributed, and which is still so much in vogue today.

Intimate gardening is not defined by surface area alone. Although most of today's examples are small, those praised by Mrs. Martineau cover a lot of ground. Two other factors count much more in determining this style: first of all the garden's mood, created by that rich, even exuberant blend of floral color and texture she so admires; and second, the way in which the garden is lived in by its owners, how it is experienced. Such domains are secluded from the outside world and receive direct, personal attention from loving owners. The result of all these elements combined is highly individual and largely informal.

Such a style also implies a special sense of time. The breakneck rhythms of life outside are slowed down to a tranquil pace which allows careful contemplation of an unfolding leaf or bloom. Paradoxically, however, although such gardens may be calm oases, they are in constant flux. Plant lovers are forever making new discoveries, trying new experiments, developing new corners.

The Riviera draws many such people precisely because its climate, or rather, its microclimates, allow the pursuit of this process all year round. It is true that most newcomers from northern spheres generally lose their first plantings because they underestimate the mistral, or summer drought (Edith Wharton already warned against that). They soon learn that it is much easier to have a Riviera garden full of flower in February than in July. But all this is a highly personal process of trial and error, a pursuit that goes on for years.

Intimate Riviera gardens may be found on a wide variety of sites. The following examples range from mountaintop to railroad gully, from the heart of Nice to a tiny enclave among much grander properties on Saint-Jean-Cap-

Ferrat, from the moist bottomland around an old mill to the ramparts of a medieval hilltown. Quite a few, and not the least original, can be found in modern suburbia. The first one, however, lies in the heart of the backcountry, at the top of Paradise Lane.

A MOUNTAIN GORGE

One of the most imaginative gardens on the Riviera today can only be reached by a steep uphill climb of several hundred meters, over a stony and often muddy mule track called, despite the rough going, Paradise Lane. And yet its owner, Bruno Goris-Poncé, has many visitors who come to admire his collections of flowering shrubs, perennials, and winter-flowering roses. He is fast becoming known as one of the best plantsmen in the region, a connoisseur who is also knowledgeable about garden design and history. His stocky figure, topped with a wide-brimmed straw hat and accompanied by his inseparable black dog, can be found in many of the Riviera's oldest and most prestigious gardens. For Monsieur Goris is a professional gardener and advisor on garden restoration.

The house he now inhabits was purchased by his grandfather who had spotted its terraces, perched on an abrupt mountain slope, from the other side of the narrow valley. They sheltered not only olive but three hundred orange trees—only two of which survived the killer frosts of 1956. Monsieur Goris's grandfather, who had won a medal during World War II for getting the German prisoners in his charge to grow vegetables, immediately set about cultivating the plot he acquired with his new property.

Monsieur Goris spent most of his vacations as a child in this house. After his grandfather's death, the property was abandoned for ten years. In 1980, Monsieur Goris began its renovation by planting trees, and was able to live here as of 1985. He added apricot, almond, and cherry trees, and replaced his grandfather's weeping willow on the house terrace with a more traditional lime. This space was enlarged for outdoor dining, extended by a grassy stretch edged by a low stone wall. The only patch of lawn in this garden, it is given over to children and dogs—a play area, as it were, but also a quiet space among the general exuberance of plants elsewhere, a void in the midst of plenitude.

The spectacularly rugged mountain wall opposite, by its very scale and proximity, posed a problem to the new gardener—what foreground plantings could do it justice? The mountain is a constant presence, shadowing visitors uphill and down from the entrance of the house to the road below (this path is also bordered with pocket spaces for more flowers and vegetables). Opposite his front door, Monsieur Goris decided to plant a border of low shrubs and high perennials around the dining area, not blocking the view, nor exactly framing it but taming it somewhat, making it another guest at dinner rather than a threat to garden intimacy.

This border was Bruno Goris's first effort at garden planting and the beginning of an

"... A little rustic seat whereon he sits when eating his simple déjeuner while a nightingale sings." Lady Fortescue, describing her neighbor in Perfume from Provence, might have written this about Bruno Goris, who dines outdoors next to a rare Abutilon morandia (bottom).

Goris's enchanting garden abounds in soft, warm welcoming tones: yellow upon yellow, soft pinks, and vibrant red (facing page).

Paradise Lane also leads to Noah's Ark: Bruno Goris loves and shelters many animal companions (above). Goris's garden contains some two hundred varieties of old roses, including many musk roses such as 'Penelope' (center).

ever-expanding garden. Having few resources, he started off, quite simply, by planting this space with whatever people gave him: box, nandina, Japanese anemones, artemisias. To find out what would survive here, he visited the Schneider sisters' nursery in Cannes with only a few francs to his name. Recognizing a kindred spirit, they took him around the whole place, explaining the needs and habits of each plant. He still refers to the sisters as the "good fairies" of the Côte d'Azur.

He has since resolved to grow only plants which are happy with his soil and climate. He cannot, he says, take time to nurture delicate additions. Today, his garden contains several thousand varieties of happy, thriving plants.

Like his grandfather, Monsieur Goris grows vegetables. He has transformed the old kitchen garden into a succession of decorative compartments, separated from each other by tall, clipped hedges made from the local hornbeam, *Ostrya carpinifolia*. All are protected by a high, stone retaining wall along the north side. A central path edged with silver santolina leads through a series of arches linking these successive separations for the whole length of the garden. The path is now being covered with a pergola sporting a 'La Follette' rose.

The first compartment contains ornamentals only, mingled in the cottage garden manner: *Pittosporum tobira* 'Nana' to outline the wall behind, tree peonies, berberis, campanulas, bronze fennel, bergenias, cistus, roses, and an ever-flowering, tall and golden "Burmese" day lily that Bruno Goris retrieved from old Riviera gardens. There is also the single-flowered golden kerria, and a variety of abutilons. The second room displays formal rows of lettuces, carrots, onions, and chard enclosed in a hedge of rosemary. The third houses taller and more spreading vegetables—tomatoes, eggplant, zucchini.

The main itinerary in the Goris garden winds uphill behind the house, below the jagged crests of the mountaintop rising at a sharp angle on this side of the valley as well. The general direction emerges only little by little. The grassy paths meander from terrace to terrace, each so densely planted (though never crowded) that one feels quite enclosed (though never smothered). At first these spaces were mown just twice yearly. Then the low retaining walls were cleared and repaired, and planted both at their base and on outer edges with flowering shrubs and perennials which would drape and fall nicely. Gradually the masses formed, and now the

walls have all but disap-
peared. Gnarled olive
trunks and spreading fruit
trees rise above the foliage
to add height here and
there. Terracotta jars are
half-buried at strategic
points. Wildflowers and
bulbs, however common-
place, are welcomed if
they are beautiful. Many
plants resow themselves
happily, and Bruno
respects these unpre-
dictable bounties. There
are some two hundred
varieties of old roses
(including the Nabonnand
tea roses again, such as

'Papa Gontier' and 'Général Schablikine');
and others, better known elsewhere—all the
moschata hybrids which here often flower in
winter. A small mountain of 'Buff Beauty'
wafts its rich scent above lower-growing but
larger-flowered blossoms of a deeper yellow.

Everything is warm in this garden. Bruno
Goris is bemused by the current fashion
which shuns reds and yellows. The latter are
present here in the blossoms of fremontodendron, *Euryops pectinatus*, cassias, Spanish
broom, and phlomis, all very much at home.
These hues correspond, he feels, to the warm
southern light. Indeed, a new garden space of
about twelve square yards is being planted
largely in whites and yellows: helianthemums
and marigolds against a carpet of starry-blue
Aphyllanthes monspeliensis as a sort of floral

representation of the celes-
tial vault, to which other
details will add echoes of
Aquarian symbolism.

Monsieur Goris's imagi-
nation is endless and it
seems that the riches of his
garden must be also. He
has become a well-known
figure at all the local plant
fairs where his unusual
contributions are much
sought after. People also
ask his advice on original
plant associations, for his
garden abounds in inven-
tive interminglings. For
example, through the
branches of a white-flow-
ered Judas tree climbs a *Clematis cirrhosa
balearica*, which has finished flowering when
its host begins. But also intertwined is a
'Pompon de Paris' rose, which covers up the
unsightly summer foliage of the clematis.

Monsieur Goris's garden is a small Eden,
and perhaps also a Noah's Ark. There are
extensive greenhouses and potting sheds, a
garden for medicinal plants only, poultry
runs not just for chickens and rabbits but
also for pheasants, turkeys, and ducks.
Pigeons have their own dovecote. On the wild
hillside above, two sheep, Nutmeg and Snowdrop, graze happily.

All living creatures coexist peacefully in
this privileged space. Monsieur Goris does
comment that male dogs have a habit of making for the boxwood, while the females make

*Cottage
garden flowers
proliferate happily in
the Goris garden: love-
in-a-mist (Nigella
damascena) self-sows
from year to year
(above). Vibrant pink
oenothera wafts its scent
through the summer air.
This rather lax
perennial has lately
become popular in
informal Riviera
gardens (center).*

holes in his plot of grass . . . but after all, this is first and foremost a garden for living in. It has been variously called "English," or a *jardin de curé*, or simply a wild garden—so many terms with which visitors try to encompass its overflowing vitality.

A MEDIEVAL HILLTOWN

Years ago, Princess Grace of Monaco described with admiration an "exquisite small garden" which "has retained the privacy and peace of a cloister by the use of minute box hedges and walls tumbling with green creepers." This garden still exists, though its creator, landscape architect Raymond Poteau, has passed away. Secretive and quite unique, it lies on three terraces below the church of a medieval hilltown, enclosed by its own high walls on both sides, but open onto the splendid vista of the countryside and the sea beyond. Three tiny village properties were patiently acquired to create this site.

A discreet door under an arch in a narrow street gives no indication of the hidden paradise beyond. The garden must be reached through the house, of which it is a natural extension. For the beige stucco building with its ocher-red curtains and shutters already occupies several levels, each looking onto the garden below. The ground-floor level has been left half open, as a winter garden, so that the transition to outdoor spaces is gradual.

From the house, one emerges onto a long terrace planted with a multitude of very low, small-scaled, box-edged compartments in intricate designs around a simple stone well. Their geometrical design is an attempt to impose order on a profusion of bright annuals, including zinnias and tall, orange-flowered cosmos. Each end of the terrace has private nooks with pots and benches, the west side hiding a small, vaulted grotto behind a raised dining platform made of old brick, with speckle-leaved *Polygonum capitatum* on the step risers. The high, rough rock of the cliff rises behind, half-covered with evergreen *Ficus pumila* and fragrant star jasmine.

Monumental cypresses stand guard at each end of this level. Viewed from below, they frame the village's church tower to the east, its castle to the west. A sculpted stone

cornice set along the outer edge of the terrace is almost smothered by an enormous, blue-flowered *Solanum rantonnettii* which dominates the garden in late summer. Two stone balls indicate the entrance to a double staircase leading to the next level down, built parallel to the retaining wall.

Between their twin ramps and only visible after descending, an elegant fountain is encased in the wall, like another small grotto, set among papyrus sprays. A vault with embedded seashells, along with a seashell face above a rounded basin on a pedestal (itself set on semi-circular steps) add a rococo note to this rustic but refined garden, which is picked up elsewhere in the curving shapes of certain beds, and other sculptural details. `

This second level constitutes the broadest space of the garden. The scale of planting, meant also to be seen from above, is much bigger. Box hedging again defines compartments, here overflowing with tree-sized oleanders, citrus of all descriptions, one low-growing palm like a fountain of fronds, roses, asters, daturas, and . . . raspberry bushes. A grape arbor runs the length of the east wall, sheltering a marble figure who seems to enjoy the view westward.

Gravel paths lead from the rococo wall fountain toward a simple glazed urn at a juncture of the box-framed compartments. Beyond, in the center of this terrace's outer edge, stands the whole composition's strongest focal point: an open V-shaped curtain of cypresses, squared off at the top, framing an antique column which in turn supports a Baroque comedy mask. It looks back at the house, inviting and mocking at the same time. This Italianate architectural feature, combining clipped greenery and sculpture, anchors the garden's lavish and colorful profusion. It is just as theatrical when viewed from the house above.

Hidden behind the cypress wall, a turquoise rectangle—the swimming pool—lies like a jewel in its paved setting. A simple fountain brings water to its east end. Square, ocher-washed columns along the terrace's outer edge support a trellis which supplies welcome shade while framing the view of the valley and sea beyond. Each column is topped by a green ceramic ball, echoing both the stone ones of similar size by the double staircase and green tiles placed elsewhere in

An exquisite, beautifully-scaled garden lies at the heart of a medieval hilltown, between castle and church. Its high walls and hedges shelter many exotics, including this tree datura (Brugmansia) with vibrant red lychnis at its foot (right).

*A marble
column supporting a
comedy mask stands out
against a dark cypress
curtain and the ever-
changing sea (following
pages).*

the garden. A 'La Follette' rose winds its way over this support.

This is a garden of perfect scale, in which both the large lines and small detailing have received careful attention. The western rim of the pool breaks its straight line with a curve jutting out over the blue water below— just enough to allow for a small oval mosaic of low-growing rockery plants (a clump of lavender, an artemisia, and a carpet of silver-leaved dimorphothecas).

Through the columns of the pergola, one can also look down on the garden's lowest terrace, narrow and enclosed in high walls but extended by the "borrowed" elements of old tiled roofs, and the sculpted décor of a pink-washed manor house nearby. It shelters two box-edged beds of shrubs (yew, summer lilac, dwarf palm) laid out in a rococo design around terracotta urns. A tall specimen of the rare tree *Chorisia insignis*, which flowers twice a year, snuggles against the rough wall of the cliff at the west end. Here a banana tree and a spiky cactus column also thrive.

From inside this space, looking back upward, one finds the high retaining wall decked with a lovely, natural intermingling of feathery *Lavandula dentata*, creeping polygonum, and deep blue-flowering Corsican rosemary—a simple, easy but most effective combination.

Rare is the garden which can blend so successfully a Mediterranean sense of design and theatrical décor (multiple perspectives from all levels to all levels) with such a prodigal display of lush, colorful bloom—all in such a small, sheltered and very intimate space. Princess Grace was right: the atmosphere is definitely one of peace and privacy, and this garden is indeed "exquisite."

Inland,
a mill stream waters this surprising domain where Mediterranean and northern inspiration combine. Liquidambars intermingle with lagerstroemia, cistus with hydrangeas. This is one of garden writer Rosemary Verey's favorite Riviera gardens.

AN OLD MILL

In the heart of a peaceful river valley where hayfields and woodlands thrive, an old mill was transformed many decades ago into an elegant residence. The present English owners have been there more than thirty years. On the surrounding slopes, *garrigue* vegetation gives way to more moisture-loving plants; indeed, the vicomte de Noailles, who advised occasionally on this property, claimed that he could locate on these hillsides the exact limit of the habitat of wild mimosa.

The owners have made the most of their special microclimate, planting a wide variety of trees for spring bloom and fall color. Catalpas, liquidambars, robinias, flowering cherries, and magnolias, now mature, surround the house and create a dense, private enclave.

The entrance road to this domain passes through an expanse of flat meadows—for the river valley spreads broadly at this point. Naturalized flowers grow here in profusion until the end of May, when the field is first mowed. The road arrives at a courtyard shaded by carefully-pruned plane trees. A pillar-box dovecote at one end is surrounded by Japanese quince and spring bulbs.

An arched gate leads through a cypress hedge into the garden proper. Against the dark curtain of the cypresses, a series of stone pillars supports different rambling roses. Beyond, a square, formal garden outlined by its stone paths is laid out around a central fountain. Well-proportioned, it serves above all as a foreground for the copse of magnolias beyond—some twelve different varieties, including *M. soulangeana* 'Lennei', *M. loebneri* 'Leonard Messel' and 'Merrill', *M. liliiflora* 'Nigra', *M. campbellii*—in shades from deep pink to palest cream, broad and narrow petals, even one with peeling bark.

To the right, this space is linked to the house by more stone arches laden with white wisteria and pink roses. Two stately plane trees shade the residence, and also shelter two fanciful box topiary some ten feet high: a rabbit and a squirrel. Other familiar spirits guard the house in the form of small sculptures, a dog's head here, a faun's face there, peeking through greenery.

Many sheltered corners here contain small-scaled plantings: a trough tumbles over with sedums and other succulents, a bright blue ceanothus happily intermingles with a lime-green *Euphorbia characias wulfenii*.

The banks of the millstream running past the house have been made into long, low terraces, accompanying a riverside walk some two hundred yards long. It is edged with the strong forms of Corsican hellebores, striking clumps of hydrangeas (*quercifolia* and *aspera villosa*) from which emerge astonishing, multitrunked summer lilacs (*Lagerstroemia indica*). Unpruned and soaring, they provide aerial swaths of white, purple, and pink blossom at the end of summer. Northern and southern vegetation blend harmoniously here in original associations: day lilies and lespedeza; albizias through which ramble the violet-blue blossoms of the climbing rose 'Rose-Marie Viaud' (similar to 'Veilchenblau'); apricot trees; two purple-leaved plums mingling with white-flowered Judas trees; exotic pineapple guava and *Vitex* (the snail or pepper bush with white or purple spikes). The oak-leaved hydrangeas are fronted by fine-leaved, pink-flowering cistus ('Peggy Sammons') and Japanese anemones. Around a small waterfall, in mottled shade and sun, hostas thrive along with agapanthus, kniphofias, white and yellow lupins, all near a large Chinese privet.

At the end of this walk, out of sight from the house, lies a round swimming pool which looks much more like a garden basin. The elegant building which rises along its far side completes the pleasant sense of enclosure.

The obvious itinerary is to walk from the

house terrace along the river path to the pool, passing many and varied plantings, then to return toward the house on a slightly higher level, through a shady arboretum of rare trees (unusual varieties of catalpa, acacia, flowering cherries including the yellow-flowered 'Yukon', and a *Davidia* or handkerchief tree). All along this walk are enjoyable views on meadows and distant hills to the east.

They can be seen even better from the wilder hillside across the river. This has been planted as woodland, but it also features tree varieties unusual for this region: more liquidambar, hydrangeas, and magnolias; golden laburnums, rare pines, deodar cedars, blue spruces, maples, and oaks. There are also more summer lilacs, white poplars, and a grove of Judas trees, again a mix of local and exceptional plantings in happy proximity.

Abundant water makes possible these unusual combinations. The property is crisscrossed by stone-edged canals designed to supply every part of the garden, and indeed the valves are opened once a week for deep irrigation.

These gardeners do not rest on their laurels—nor their magnolias. New areas are developed yearly. A recent wrought-iron *gloriette* by the pool will soon be covered by 'Clair Matin' roses, white wisteria, Japanese clematis as well as *montana rubens* and 'Mrs. Cholmondeley'. The garden will provide fragrant retreats, perhaps for the daughter of the house to play her flute. For this is a family garden, where everyone participates. It is rather larger than other examples considered here, but its intimacy comes from the comfortable sense of enclosure around the millstream, from the division of its space into a series of welcoming rooms densely planted with many different colors and textures, and from its owners' obvious warm, personal involvement.

This family takes delight in original plant associations which here, given their garden's size, can include trees. Many plant collectors on the Riviera yearn to succeed with delicate tropical plants. The owners of the mill garden extend their limits not toward the equator but to the north. In a Côte d'Azur setting, northern exoticism is perhaps even more difficult to achieve—but equally justifiable, after all, in a region where individual fancy in its infinite variety long ago became the essence of regional style.

A SEASIDE CITADEL

The unspoiled coastline of the Var department east of Hyères, backed by rolling vineyards around small châteaux and hilltowns, is becoming increasingly popular for summer residences. One contemporary house sits on a wild summit just a few steps from the sea, easily reached through a grove of wind-bent pines. Built from limestone slabs on the site of a former quarry, it has an unusual semicircular form around a paved courtyard. There is a partial second storey on the east side, and the garden extends out from the bedrooms contained by this upper level—a broad swath of lawn echoing the curves of the house. It is thus a suspended garden, enclosed by pines and a high wall on the horizon to the east, giving onto dazzling sea views of inlets, islands, and distant promontories to the west.

The long, curving access from west to east on the upper storey, a narrow passage between waist-high stone walls, resembles nothing so much as the sentry round of some medieval battlements. Indeed, one square stone tower rises to further the comparison. Looking from here across the courtyard to the main part of the garden, one has a lovely general view of both the intimate nooks and corners sheltered by the house, and the wider, larger scaled plantings curving up the hill. At this same west end of the "sentry round," the low stone balustrade supports a long expanse of the Mermaid rose.

This is a domain in which a great variety of crisscrossing perspectives has been carefully planned, making the most of the semicircular layout of the building. Already, the level surrounding the lower courtyard has large windows on both sides, partially shaded by the overhang of the level above, all creating shifting light effects according to season and time of day. More dappled effects are created by the parasol branches of a carefully pruned mulberry tree in the heart of the courtyard. Against the north wall, a strong, dark cypress column links the two storeys, while on the east side a particularly beautiful, gnarled olive tree spreads its crown over two playful topiary geese on the ground

This seaside garden was created level with the upper storey of its house, its terracotta paving actually serving as roof to rooms around a courtyard below. Driftwood and semi-wild plants like cistus (rockrose) echo the nearby beach (center and following pages).

below. The very crown of this tree, which reaches the parapet wall of the garden above, has been pruned into a flat band level with the stone ridge.

Stone, wood, and vegetation constantly intermingle, just as house and garden form one inseparable unit. Rarely indeed is wood put to so many different ornamental uses in southern gardens. The "sentry round" passage of the upper storey is supported by two stone arches to the west and by heavy wooden beams to the east. The same weathered beams provide vertical supports for the loggias of the second storey. From here, a wooden trellis extends outward, the rough bark of its uprights barely distinguishable from the vine trunk it supports. In the garden itself, fine pieces of driftwood sit among the plantations, one set vertically so that its vestigial branches invite birds to perch. The high beds which form the eastern horizon line of the garden are supported not only by a curved, stone retaining wall but also by barrel staves set upright (naturally enough, since this gardener is also the owner of the Domaine de Maleherbe, a prestigious wine-producing property near Bormes-les-Mimosas). Each end of the sloping lawn in the upper garden is closed off by a rustic, wooden gate.

The garden is like a concentration of the surrounding wilderness, including native plants and echoes of both mountains and sea (sailors' lanterns also hang on the house walls). Within its enclave, however, growth is carefully controlled by a watchful eye and a skillful hand. A pine sheltering the trellised patio has its growth points nipped regularly, making it into a large-scale bonsai. The effect is not strained, for the owner is inspired by the naturally produced "bonsais" of the maritime landscapes—small, ancient trees whose roots find bare sustenance between two layers of rock by the windswept shore.

Within the limits of her garden, she has incorporated a stand of cork oaks, pruning them just so that their trunks stand dramatically silhouetted against a curtain of variegated ivy. At their feet, three small topiary sheep frolic on the lawn, perhaps planning to drink at the small round pond nearby. The driftwood terrace is a sand garden supporting a silver tower of *Anthyllis barba-jovis* (found wild in some parts of the coast here but rare and protected), a miniature white asphodel, two *Dorycniums* or lotus (*D. hirsutum*, and *D. suffruticosus* syn. *pentaphyllus*), spurges, and many bulbs including sand lilies, cistus, and daisy-flowered olearias. Cryptomeria, creeping

spurges, and sedums are allowed to sow themselves everywhere. Cistus are found in every part of the garden, echoing their natural wild habitat even as they provide the variety of rare garden cultivars. Junipers, heathers, arbutus, myrtles, and terebinths all recall the local seaside vegetation, but are present here in choice varieties. Roses too are selected for their soft hues and wild aspect. One of the prettiest plants is the round-leaved *Carissa*, in both the upright and dwarf forms.

Colors here are always soft and carefully managed. A pale yellow, simple-flowered abutilon with a more deeply hued center is fronted by a clump of late daffodils with the same tones. A two-foot high thistle, *Galac-*

Pittosporum crassifolium guard the steps. Clumps of silver artemesias, *Senecio* 'White Diamond' and creeping chrysanthemum (*C. haradjanii*) intermingle with rarities, such as a white "sage" or *Ozothamnus*. Throughout the garden, rust-red, succulent clumps of aeoniums set off other silver and green foliage.

The seaside climate imposes certain constraints—all of these plants must resist salt air, of course. Their limestone setting makes snails a constant problem. But at the same time, the garden enjoys heavy dew much of the year, even when inland areas are dried up.

Seagulls whirl overhead, their circles repeating the garden's own curves. Although circular rather than square, this unusual site recalls the cloisters of medieval monasteries,

Many Riviera gardens marry stone and vegetation, but this one on the sea also gives a large place to weathered wood. Barrel staves support the planting bed, while wooden gates enclose the garden at both ends.

tites tomentosa, is covered with pale rose bloom in spring. The main focal point of the hillside sloping up from the house is a raised bed opposite the trellised patio, beyond the swath of lawn, right in the heart of the garden. Here two leaning pine trunks back a smoky-pink tamarisk, flowering at the same time as the more delicate pink rhaphiolepis, and deep blue echium candles. Color, texture, and shape have all been carefully orchestrated. This May picture replaces an earlier one on the same spot in March, rich with freesias and a billowy white exochorda, now discreet in the shadow of the tamarisk.

In the series of small, irregular, paved spaces near the house, plant texture is even denser, the scale smaller, the number of treasures in pots increased. Twin, plump

planned for the communion of earth and heaven, microcosms of the outside, natural state improved by art. Here house, garden, landscape, and seascape all form one harmonious—and intimate—enclave.

A SUBURBAN PLOT

A very different tapestry of plants has been created overlooking one of the Riviera's largest cities and the bay beyond. Marie-Thérèse Haudebourg and her family occupy a corner house on a long triangle of ground sloping steeply south. Enclosed by high walls and cypress hedging on three sides, the garden circles round the house, opening southward onto the sea view. Carefully planned, it seems much larger than it really is.

Madame Haudebourg is a designer as much as a collector: she loves plants for themselves, she says, and not for their rarity. But she is also very much a plantswoman, well known to readers of the magazine *Mon Jardin Ma Maison* for her knowledgeable advice column on Côte d'Azur gardening. An expert on southern varieties of old roses, she is currently preparing a reference book on the subject for Les Editions Hachette.

One enters through a gate at the northeast corner, where a broad stretch of lawn sets off borders of shrubs and perennials on both sides (a wide variety of sages and solanums, allogynes, phygelius, creeping rosemaries, silver-leaved convolvulus, verbenas, the yellow blooms of *Bidens ferilifolia*,

western limit. This short, shady section creates yet another set of growing conditions, another microclimate, for different experiments. Perennial *Geranium sanguineum* intermingles with dimorphotheca 'Buttermilk', while the strongly defined, lime-green shapes of *Helleborus foetidus* emerge from a carpet of pale blue felicia, surrounded by a swath of *Anemone blanda*. Another oak, and a newly planted lime tree shade the main outdoor eating space in the southwest corner.

The swimming pool occupies almost all the space south of the house, but its retaining walls support densely planted beds which can again be examined in detail from below (white violets running among magenta sage, creeping *Eriocephalus*, and a very pretty,

and much more). A small orange tree sports its golden globes against the lavender-blue shutters of the beige stuccoed house. A row of olive trees leads along the top (north) side of the property, one of which displays the yellow blooms of a 'Madame Pierre S. Dupont' climbing rose.

A spreading oak stands as a majestic focal point at the far end, guarding the entrance to a rockery on a rise of ground in the northeast corner (*Cheiranthus* 'Bowles Hybrid' here mingles with *Cistus* 'Peggy Sammons'). Opposite the rock garden, a row of six espaliered pear trees is nearly smothered by the pale pink-flowering, fragrant pelargoniums at their feet. These tumble into one of two sunken patios tucked into corners of the house, leading downhill along the property's

pink-blossomed oenothera among them). A narrow path leads past an iris collection to a row of tree peonies. Here a winter-flowering, heavenly-scented *Buddleja officinalis* supports a lespedeza which will bloom in summer, when the buddleja is dull.

The path then winds up a rise along the eastern edge of the property, under windbent pines, past low shrubbery to the house's main entrance. Here plants in pots are effectively grouped by the door (fatsia set off by silver cineraria, for example). Opposite, where the ground falls away toward the road outside, is a shaded, moist corner under the pines, where Madame Haudebourg has just put in a pond, beloved by the local bird population. One great, dramatic clump of broadleaved, white-flowered sparmannia masks

Marie-Thérèse Haudebourg makes expert use of colors and volumes to create the illusion of a much larger garden. Each side of the house has its own atmosphere, created by dense and thoughtful plantings, here a 'Cécile Brunner' rose, euryops, and Solanum rantonnettii.

Madame Haudebourg's garden, like Madame Guillermin's, has been enriched by many friendly exchanges with other enthusiasts. The former prefers soft colors, the latter collects bright abutilons and roses including 'Paul's Scarlet Climber' (above) and 'Lauré Davoust' (center).

this hollow from the gate. And thus one has come full circle.

So it is that this small garden has been organized into a succession of very distinct spaces, each with different conditions of exposure and moisture, each full of specially adapted plants. Madame Haudebourg does not always agree with established opinion on the best conditions for each: she finds for example that the pineapple-scented sage, *Salvia elegans*, grows best in shade, where it can assume enormous proportions. White fuchsias, in her garden, thrive in the sun.

Her great speciality is original plant associations. She often walks around the garden, flowers in hand, trying out new mixtures. The vibrant, cerise flowers of *Salvia buchananii* she sets off with silver foliage plants. The shrubby China rose *odorata* 'Sanguinea' is flanked by the ever-flowering *Lavandula dentata*. A great fountain of deep blue *Solanum rantonnettii* grows next to rigid, yellow daisy-flowered *Euryops pectinatus* and the velvety, mauve and white spikes of *Salvia leucantha*. This is all underplanted with pale mauve lantana and set against a stand of her favorite rose-red salvia. She manages beautifully seasonal transitions: one space displays white bleeding hearts in spring (*Dicentra alba*), which will fade away under a covering of pale blue plumbago in late summer. At the same time, she also lets chance take a hand: throughout the property, rustic varieties of simple-flowered chrysanthemums have sown themselves happily, providing touches of old rose, pale yellow, or an unusual pinky-white of a variety which changes color as it ages. It mingles happily with the deep blue of a Corsican rosemary, flowering at the same time.

Clearly, this is a garden of subtle color blends. Madame Haudebourg claims her favorite is pink, and that she dislikes orange. She makes full use, however, of primary hues with a sure eye for tonal compatibility. She employs in particular different yellows to set off almost anything else—a lesson for those who fear yellow as a garden color. As for her garden's design, one may say that she has created what Russell Page describes as that "subtle and deliberate disorder that softens the emphasis of a straight line and never allows the garden to appear static or achieved."

TREASURE TROVES

Intimate gardening gives rise to those "over-the-back-fence" friendships which promote plant exchanges and gardening gossip. Marie-

Thérèse Haudebourg's magazine column transfers this practice into print, keeping much the same spirit. She has also become a friendly advisor to the nearby nursery of Mediterranean specialties run by the Bonaut family. Such plantsmen's networks are far more active and growing on the French Riviera than is generally suspected, a kind of horticultural underground that emerges regularly at local plant fairs.

Bruno Goris is also the center of such a network. One of his many contacts is Madame Guillermin, a retired lady who gardens at the foot of Paradise hill in a former railroad gully. The entire slope was long ago built up as a series of very steep, narrow terraces. Those rising above her garden still sport their original plantations of olive trees.

A big albizia and a walnut tree shade part of Madame Guillermin's haven, but most of it lies in full sun. Everything flourishes in a riot of color. A pale yellow abutilon spreads happily against a mass of purple bougainvillea (which Colette called "floral lava"). Huge clumps of the purple orchid *Bletilla striata*, other red-flowered and variegated abutilons, many sages including the giant, dark blue S. *guaranitica*, candles of red and yellow kniphofia, cascades of sky-blue plumbago, smoky fountains of fennel, pools of pale yellow coreopsis, some two thousand tulips, a classic 'La Follette' rose threading through a cypress, pittosporums, sparmannias, pomegranate trees, oleanders, and mixed beds of anthemis in numerous varieties make this very carefully tended and obviously much-loved treasure trove appear like an overflowing casket of jewels displayed by the side of a country road.

The effect from within is even more intoxicating, since the house, a transformed railroad shelter, is somewhat sunken in relation to its approachways. The tall, pale gray stone retaining walls which rise behind provide the right sense of intimate enclosure. They also, of course, double the surface area of the domain. Indeed, these small collectors' havens make use of every square inch to maximum capacity.

Madame Guillermin gets most of her plants as cuttings from friends, and rarely fails to make them grow. Unusual items mix with the commonplace in a profusion of fruit and flower—all waifs are welcome. But however dense the planting, she knows that her wealth of plants is always structured by the strong lines of the terracing, and sheltered by the warmth of its walls. Indeed, the site benefits from unusual protection: her orange

trees were the only ones in the locality to survive the frosts of 1985.

In such gardens, profusion and abundance sometimes win out entirely over design. The sequence can be a bit haphazard because, where everything is a treasure, there is no concern for precedence. Owners of these properties usually state at the outset that they are not "real" gardeners, but collectors, at the mercy of a fascination which can become a real addiction. Such places have a magic of their own which derives from the love their creators feel for their protégés. They are havens quite literally, and the plants respond gratefully.

Another unusually rich garden sits near Le Bar-sur-Loup on a steep hillside, on the edge of a housing development. Its owners, a retired couple, are first of all active orchid lovers. Part of their living room has been transformed into a winter garden to house fragile species. Outdoors, their great passion is subtropical plants of all kinds.

The property was purchased in 1976 as a vacation home, and the garden begun in 1980. When they were able to move here all year round, the owners happily set out all the plants which they had grown in a greenhouse in Alsace. That winter they

had 1.5 feet of snow. Everything began again. Today they manage a series of jungle landscapes, starting at the entrance, where an old olive tree has been surrounded, if not invaded, by luxuriant climbers like *Solandra hartwegii* with its huge, tulip-shaped yellow blooms, various passion flowers and jasmines, kiwi vines, and deep red roses. The itinerary leads downhill through pergolas of perpetual-flowering *Jasminum azoricum* to a series of small-scaled, narrow terraces, each supporting a different garden. Palms and agaves and yuccas in all varieties punctuate the descent.

On one level, water from the swimming pool spills over into fountains filled with lotus. Two lower levels have been reserved for elegantly arranged vegetable plantings. At the end of another, a greenhouse maintained at 15° centigrade protects a collection of tropical *Bromeliaceae*, a stunning pelican flower vine (*Aristolochia grandiflora*), a rare *Passiflora quandrangularis*, and various carnivorous plants. Another terrace has been

transformed into a miniature marsh, the foot of an ancient olive tree protected by hidden plastic from the damp ground beneath.

Steps link all these terraces at either end, making it possible to zigzag down the hill, but each one has also been planned separately around a central path. At different points, small hexagonal wooden structures perch like gazebos, but each in fact functions as a glasshouse for still more tropical plants. And if these were not riches enough, another level ends with a large birdhouse, the bright colors of its inhabitants competing with those of the surrounding flowers.

To return to the house, one climbs back up to the pool area past a series of small ponds with water gardens, where a variety of fish, including carp, enjoy the same care as the plants and birds. By the swimming pool, a rare corner of lawn is flanked by more local plants, a Judas tree, a cypress, and a blue-spiked echium.

A trip through this garden seems to lead through several continents, and at least half a dozen different landscapes—all dominated by the spectacular blue mountains rising across the valley. And all contained on only 2500 square meters of land!

Differences of level allow for particularly dramatic displays, but another retiree has managed to transform a small, flat plot of land into an equally brilliant paradise. This garden in the heart of Saint-Jean-Cap-Ferrat, is surrounded by magnificent and sometimes legendary domains (Somerset Maugham's property is just around the corner).

The owner, who has been living here permanently since 1979, built a simple, modern villa in the middle of his plot, and has given careful thought to its organization. Finding himself without enough room for his more than five hundred species and varieties, and not having retaining walls to double the space, he makes the most of pots. These he places among the plants which are growing directly in the ground, and sometimes piles them up for display on planters at different levels. At the same time, he has carefully designed flagstone and gravel paths through the garden, lined with pots of course, to make the most of benches and viewpoints, planting to frame views. The statue of an Arlesienne woman emerges from one shrub grouping, an old-fashioned street lamp from

Collectors on a mountain slope have extended their plant range by creating a series of artificial settings. Here a miniature marsh lies below the canopy of an olive tree. The latter's foot is protected by buried plastic.

another. His lot has preserved a few one hundred-year-old pines, but the perspectives are further abetted by the majestic cypresses and pine canopies of the far grander properties which surround him.

In the heart of his magic circle, this gentleman has created a well of intense color which has its best vantage point from the balcony of the pale, stuccoed, turquoise-shuttered villa. A round pond just below is edged with still more pots. Collections of iris and hibiscus; many bright, semitropicals like the red and blue *Tibouchina*; and spreading vines like *Thunbergia* grow in abundance. By way of example: just the few square meters by the entrance gate contain a shrubby *Fothergilla*; bunches of Kaffir lilies; spreading, purple-blue jacaranda and a pink-blossomed albizia tree; half-hardy, daisy-flowered olearias; and climbing *Kennedya*. And more still: to fill every space of his 1100-square-meter property, the gardener resorts to bedding plants!

Sometimes the plant passion leads to professional involvement, when an owner has a gift not only for discovering rarities but reproducing them. This is the case for Monsieur Dino Pellizzaro, whose family garden is laid out like a cascading rockery in the hills above Vallauris, where elegant villas still mingle with the greenhouses of commercial producers (whose terraces of vegetables and flowers can also be highly decorative).

The son of an Italian immigrant mason, Monsieur Pellizzaro took cuttings of everything in sight even as a child, trying to multiply the plants claimed to be most difficult. Today his home sits comfortably in the middle of a profusion which is both a commercial nursery and family garden, spilling over with flowers of every description. The public may inspect a wide variety of thriving plants *in situ* before choosing in the nursery. It is one of the richest—and most colorful—hoards in the country. Greenhouses below contain exotic collections, all reproduced by Monsieur Pellizzaro.

Paths winding upward need careful treading past the crowds of pots bearing plants at every stage of development. Self-sown, scarlet *Russelia* spurts out of all the stone retaining walls. The much sought-after white poppy, *Romneya coulteri*, has also

spread here and there. Many people come seeking summer flowering plants and Monsieur Pellizzaro can recommend a number of reliable, little-known ones such as *Billbergia nutans*, with drooping pink flowers, from spring to autumn, or *Fuchsia arborea* (or *mexicana*) which is the focal point in his own garden. But he stresses that summer dormancy is natural in this climate, urging customers who live here year-round to experiment with bloom in other seasons. Many very beautiful bulbs and tubers disappear in summer, like the deep blue *Scilla peruviana*, or like *Canarina canariensis*, its orange bells streaked with red. He proposes the traditional white broom (*Genista monosperma* newly renamed *Retama*); the great range of the blue, pink, or white-spiked echiums; or the small shrub *Sollya heterophylla* with its blue bellflowers for use as a groundcover. His catalogue contains much information about growing conditions, and the choice seems endless: seventy-three new additions in 1992 alone.

Monsieur Pellizzaro is specializing more and more in drought-resistant plants, collecting samples from Australia and California, seeing in this the style of the future for Mediterranean regions. His activities are gradually extending into garden planning in response to customer queries. Indeed, he can advise on which kind of lawn will thrive, without watering, as an underplanting for olive trees; or for those drawn to the northern exoticism, which kinds of Japanese maples will flourish in limy soil. Thus he pursues his passion in the heart of this small paradise where it seems everything he touches turns to green—or gray, a better color for dry climate foliage. His children seem to thrive among his other treasures, unaware perhaps of their father's distinction as a plant wizard.

Many other examples of small, collectors' gardens might be cited: Madame Perrier, author of a small book on irises for La Maison Rustique publishers, has developed collections of this plant as well as peonies and hemerocallis which were begun a generation ago by her father, many imported from America. In the stone-paved paths of her thirty-year-old garden, the shrubby *Romnya coulteri* has become an invasive weed. Another collector's garden is found at the well-named Villa Arcadie near Grasse.

At Dino Pellizzaro's nursery in Vallauris, scarlet Russelia juncea *has sown itself spontaneously in stone walls all over the property, here near a lemon tree and pink* Campanula takeïsmenia. *The Pellizzaros specialize in drought-resistant plants.*

The steep rockery leading up to the Pellizzaros' home, in the very heart of their nursery, displays some of their favorites: osteospermum and delosperma, Lavandula stoechas, and tree or Mexican fuchsia.

Here once more, small-scaled terraces present her collections in tiers like a candy shop window display. Meandering paths move from the shade of mature trees to the sunniest, most sheltered spots. This is also true of the Heysers' mountain site behind Nice in a modern housing development. Their winter garden lies on one side of the hedge-enclosed plot; on the other, where the hillside falls away, is an extensive rockery full of rare finds, and two lime trees where blackbirds come back to nest year after year.

All these collectors' gardens stand out for the quality of their plants and the originality of their conceptions. Their owners' lives revolve around them. Visitors are welcomed, if they come sharing the same passion. Indeed, if to a landscape architect these gardens' design may lack definition, if to a garden aesthete their mix of colors may lack distinction, their owners count among the most generous and enthusiastic people in the country.

A BACKCOUNTRY RETREAT

One such garden which is becoming quite famous was created by two plant lovers who married partly because of this shared passion. At first, they rented 2500 square meters in Martigues, with an agreement to stay fifteen years. Like many newcomers, they thought sun meant warmth, but underestimated winter hazards—in this case, the mistral. Wiser but still willing to experiment, they then invested in seven acres at an altitude of 350 meters in the hills behind Draguignan. Here, as in Martigues, there were

olive terraces, but the land is so protected that these trees had survived the killer frosts of 1956. Most important for the couple's purposes, there was more abundant rainfall.

Together, they first planted the descent from the road to the newly built house. The rest of the garden developed bit by bit as of 1979. At first they tended it during vacations; more recently they have been able to provide full-time care. Today three acres of their property is maintained, although, in their enthusiasm, they expand every year into new nooks and corners.

The house patio is shaded by a huge loquat, the walls decked with a violet *Hardenbergia comtoniana* and a coral vine. The main garden area consists of three parallel terraces about one hundred yards long, extending out from the house and punctuated, as is the entire hillside, by old olive trees. The narrow, middle terrace is covered with a pergola (here wood supports on strong, stone columns) and one can see its special climbers from the level above—several different honeysuckles, wisterias, bignonias, and jasmines among them, plus even rarer choices such as *Gelsemium sempervirens* and *Correa speciosa*. The terraces above and below have grassy, curving, open central spaces which invite slow strolling. Dense plantings of trees, shrubs, perennials and bulbs on either side create intimacy. These owners belong to the school which holds that bright colors suit southern light. But they are equally fascinated by the structures and textures of different plant families. This garden enthusiastically embraces variety in all of its modes.

The plantations in the heart of the garden are drought-resistant. Since these three levels were planted eight to ten years ago, before the owners moved in permanently, they were designed to survive without watering. The grass, for example, is a special, drought-resistant lawn mixture created by friends at the nursery Pépinières de la Foux.

Within this framework, almost all the plants are species, with only a few hybrids and cultivars. This is the epitome of the garden where each individual plant has been chosen for its unique qualities, and often there is only one of each. Certain families are particularly well-represented, however: more than twenty-eight species and varieties of cistus, and the same number of ceanothus, have been planted on the property.

These owners belong to many botanical societies and buy their seed all over the world. They specialize in climbers: passion flowers, jasmines, and bignonias, including the particularly unusual, pale violet *Clytostoma callistegioides*. And rarities such as *Holmskioldia sanguinea*, with its red-orange flowers from the Himalayas, or *Dipogon lignosus*, with purple-pink pea flowers, from South Africa. Seeds for the evergreen dogwood, *Cornus capitata*, came from a garden in Kyoto, pips for the pale pink rose 'Pru' came from England. At the same time, however, the owners cherish many local wild flowers.

As with all plant enthusiasts, their garden is never done. At the end of the three terrace walks, a vault will soon be made of cypresses and rambling roses. Already, a tall conifer grouping provides a strong focal point and foreground for the valley view. Where the terraces merge in the distance, a new rock garden area extends the garden onto stonier soil. Here *Nylandia*, which looks like a heather but belongs to the Polygalaceae family, intermingles with bronze fennel; a pretty, native, wild anemone; ordinary wallflowers; an unusual creeping *Erodium pelargonifolium*; pink-flowered phlomis, and much more. Two new borders, one blue and one yellow, are just being planted, as is a laundry area: here a clothesline strung between three olive trees must be surrounded by fragrant plants, but nothing prickly!

This garden has many small flowering trees, such as fragrant *Exochorda*, several types of mimosa; and buddlejas with wide, woolly leaves. Some trees reach out to the north, like the corkscrew hazelnut, dogwoods, and flowering cherries; others have southern affinities: grevilleas, olearias, and shrubby sophoras. Many of the typical cottage garden plants appear here in special forms: *Spiraea* x *bumalda* 'Crispa', or a funny, furry variety of lavender (*Lavandula lanata*). There is also a shrub gooseberry with fuchsia-like flowers.

Below the house, the former vegetable terraces have been transformed into a series of secret, experimental gardens: one for acid-loving plants mingles heathers with phygelius and passion flowers, azaleas with delphiniums. The olive tree which shades these unusual bedfellows has been protected, at its foot, from the special conditions it would not appreciate. Another corner is given over to winter-flowering bulbs.

Although the mountain view beyond is beautiful, it remains far less compelling than the delicate detailing of the highly varied foreground. At the same time, however, these gardens sit comfortably in their site, and are not at war with it. It is partly this balance which creates a strong atmosphere of general well-being. Mostly, however, this results from the owners' capacity for delight at the discovery of yet another new color nuance, or shape, or texture, in the infinite world of plants. In some respects, such collectors are the Riviera equivalent of the traditional English cottage gardeners.

SOUTHERN COTTAGE GARDENS

If many such gardens belong to transplanted northerners who retire to the south, an indigenous tradition exists as well. Genuine peasant gardens can still be found in odd corners, even on the French Riviera. Southern-born Nicole Arboireau, in Fréjus, has made a point of seeking them out, preserving old, sometimes unnamed plant varieties and organizing exchanges among enthusiasts. At the same time, she advises residents of modern apartment complexes how to start up even the smallest garden, so that neighbors may meet neighbors and the traditions of country gardening be maintained, even in such unlikely terrain.

Madame Arboireau tells the story of a southern "cottage gardener," a grandmother presiding over her plot of mixed flowers and vegetables, who pointed with pride at an unusual variety of the tall-growing squill, *Urginea maritima* (much resembling eremurus when in flower; large clumps may be seen at the Villa Noailles, or the Chèvre d'Or gardens). Remembering the bursting of the Fréjus dam in 1959, this owner explains that the plant appeared after the ensuing flood, known locally as a quasi-mythical character called *Mal passé*. "C'est Mal passé qui l'a amené," she says philosophically. The same gardener carefully plants fragrant jasmine on the edge of her plot which gives onto a campground, so that visiting vacationers can get a whiff as they go by. Madame Arboireau is fascinated by all aspects of plant lore. She can tell you that the melon-sized bulbs of this rare squill were used by the Greeks to border their fields, and were fertility symbols. She knows how to make liqueur from myrtle berries or violets, but she also knows just which wallflower will, she claims, grow only on the Roman ruins of Fréjus and nowhere else (*Antirrhinum tenuifolium*).

Plants were already her passion even as she was growing up in the nearby

town of Saint-Raphaël. Her childhood home was a typical square villa built about 1880 with some three thousand meters of abandoned parkland, where she discovered the sights, smells, and sounds of its orange plantations, its old roses, yellow jasmines, and exochorda, its pergola smothered with the climbing rose 'La Follette', its eucalyptus which "mewed" in the wind.

Madame Arboireau now gardens in a suburb near Fréjus, on a steep hillside of walled terraces where santolina-edged paths, laid out by her husband, wind round the house on several levels. Most will not admit two people abreast, and are mainly intended to let the gardener care for her rich collection of plants. Many of these are grown for fra-

different echiums. A collection of small cacti in pots sits on a painted metal table at one turning. Sometimes a wooden trellis assists the span of climbing plants over the path. Many different sages add brilliance just at the moment when the deciduous trees of surrounding woodland have their fall colors (a small, blue-flowered variety is set against the flame of Virginia creeper, under the gray-green of olive foliage). As in most of these gardens, terracotta pots provide focal points, large ones half-sunken into the ground, small ones moved about for seasonal accent, such as a scarlet fuchsia at the top of steps down from the patio. The house itself is typically besieged by tiers of plants, its terraces and verandas a pretext for more exuberant and happy layering.

Nicole Arboireau's densely planted garden in Fréjus descends in circular paths under the feathery foliage of a pepper tree. The garden has progressed bit by bit over ten years, her husband working on the masonry as she expands her sensitive selection of plants.

grance, such as a special tansy (*Tanacetum basalmita*). A rock garden brims over with kitchen herbs in their less common variants. She also specializes in local rarities: wild oleanders, for example, like the very old ones which grow beside the stream at the bottom of her hill, and the native vitex, both shrubs which developers are fast eradicating.

A good selection of trees helps her create special microclimates: an enormous false pepper tree (*Schinus molle*) shades the house terrace; farther down, more common laurels, pines, apple and Judas trees, and eucalyptus.

The low retaining walls of these small terraces allow close inspection of many large, happy clumps: spilling magenta-flowered lespedeza near upright *Euryops pectinatus*, pale lilies grouped with the furry blue candles of

Today Madame Arboireau works for the town of Fréjus, through the Municipal Tourist Office, teaching schoolchildren about plants, organizing garden clubs for the elderly, designing garden itineraries for visitors, setting up workshops for plant discovery and skills. She and her fellow gardeners take an active part in the restoration of the imposing Villa Aurélia, now municipal property, once the residence of the Murville family. (As late as the 1960s, the latter used to have cut flowers sent up to Paris daily from the Villa Aurélia gardens). Here Madame Arboireau would like to establish a garden for the five senses among the old roses, jasmines, rivers of spring bulbs, and low borders of evergreen *Myrsine africana*. Every April, she organizes the Fleuriades, a highly successful plant fair on these premises.

Nicole Arboireau's enthusiasm has led to many fruitful exchanges, and her generosity is such that she regularly sets a basket of rooted cuttings at her gate with a sign: "Help yourself."

A ROCK-STREWN OAK FOREST

Intimate gardening as practiced by modest but passionate collectors might seem to stand opposed to the world of professional landscape architects, and in theory, they appear to represent two completely different garden conceptions. In practice, however, they often overlap. Russell Page himself learned to garden as a child thanks to such collectors, "a whole world of modest flower addicts," as he

scaled, island plantings along the road, mixed with the old cork oaks of the original forest. On the other side of the house, they support the swimming pool and are strikingly visible from below.

Foresight on practical matters is another advantage of taking professional advice when making a garden: Loup de Viane refused to undertake this project unless the owners installed automatic watering in the heart of the garden. At the time, they thought him most unreasonable, but are now very grateful.

This couple has settled here to retire after many travels and adventures, and are loving every minute of it. The modern house was built on the spot where the husband found himself resting every time he went to clear the

Most of Madame Arboireau's paths will not admit two people abreast, and are mainly intended to let her care for her rich and colorful collections—here Agapanthus umbellatus.

put it. Owners who start with a professionally designed garden often fall in love with the result, getting deeply involved in its progress and evolution.

On a hilltop west of Saint-Paul-de-Vence lies a garden largely designed by Loup de Viane, a talented landscaper who has greatly influenced Riviera gardens. Its owners have of course made modifications and will make more, as this garden too is always in a state of becoming. But the original design is strong and unchangeable—particularly insofar as its layout involved the harmonious placement of huge, limestone boulders excavated when the swimming pool was dug. Loup de Viane personally supervised the exact positioning of each one, as though they were so many pieces of garden sculpture. They now define large-

brush. The swimming pool was dug out just in front of the house, on a slightly lower level. A miniature rockery links the two, and its subtle blends of foliage tone and texture still bear Loup de Viane's signature: green and black ophiopogons, spurges, dwarf box globes, ballotas; heathers; variegated podragarias; creeping verbenas; pale, creeping asters and bright, pink-flowered polygonums, intermingled with small cotoneasters and ivies in the shade of the massive oak which dominates this part of the garden. Marking the juncture of steps and pool on the far side, a large earthenware pot contains nothing but a sculpted boxwood tower—very banal, feared the owners, but they now agree it makes a telling accent. Below these steps, *Olea fragrans* provides bursts of scent in season.

This garden can be enjoyed year-round because its color depends on foliage contrasts even more than on flowers. Through the branches of the ancient oak's shady canopy twines a Virginia creeper, providing sheets of flame in the fall. Its blaze complements the subtler shades of *Vitis coignetiae* and dark, evergreen star jasmine on the house façade, the latter also offering its perfume over a long period.

At the other end of the long house terrace overlooking the pool, a smaller oak shades a formally clipped block of hebes and arbutus, making a gradual transition from the low rockery to the more open spaces beyond, while giving the terrace itself a cosy sense of enclosure. All of this contrasts beautifully with the spectacular view directly opposite. On a clear day, one can see Mougins, Valbonne, Vallauris, La Napoule, Cannes, and Antibes. This vista is underscored by a simple, bright green line: a squared-off pittosporum hedge along the pool's far side.

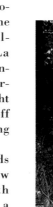

The path which leads downhill, circling below the pool, is edged with more fragrant plants: a hedge of heady-scented elaeagnus gives way to a bank of purple-leaved Chinese honeysuckle, above a hillside of cistus and red centranthus. The boulders stacked above explode with bright and fragrant coronilla in April, banked with iris and gold-edged agaves, leading to a single, billowing smokebush (*Cotinus coggygria*) at the juncture of two paths.

Continuing down, one discovers a minigolf course; a greenhouse full of cuttings; a row of great compost bins (a carefully studied design with chimneys in the middle); a vegetable plot; and the wilder, lower reaches under ancient olive trees.

The area east of the house has not yet been fully developed, and efforts to do so have had to confront the regular visits of voracious wild boars. Only on the Riviera can owners seeking the self-reliance of country living be equally endangered by both housebreakers and wild boar.

AN ELEGANT CITY COURTYARD

Absolutely different are two gardens created by Jean Mus. Although this designer has a certain palette of plants that he likes to use

regularly (lavenders, rosemaries, myrtles, cistus and dwarf pittosporums, certain roses, vittidinia and polygonum in small corners, nandinas, and of course above all the majestic olive tree), his gardens are not repetitive. Each has its own character, very much determined by the site and the taste of its owners.

Jean Mus imagined in the heart of Nice a very private courtyard garden which is quite unique. Walled in on all sides, it is a study in formal patterns which change with shifting hours and seasons. Foliage texture plays an important role, both for its intrinsic shapes and its ability to reflect or absorb light.

This garden's best vantage points are from the corner entrance gate, from the wide, white balustraded balcony that runs the length of the façade of the turn-of-the-century-style villa, and from the far corner opposite the gate, a paved patio where there is now a small barbecue. The sunlit balcony is situated at the garden's heart, underplanted with fragrant jasmine. Directly opposite, theatrically presented to the audience in the house, is a pond framed with particularly striking swords and circles: dwarf fan palms and fat, shiny-leaved *Ligularia tussilaginea*. Two much taller palms (*Chamaerops excelsa*) provide strong verticals and a patterned foliage canopy on the far side of the pond.

Everything is a play on perspectives through changing light and shade, cool and warm colors—the latter provided by well-placed terracotta pots, and a mauve bougainvillea, as old as the house, which now runs through three properties. The only bit of lawn lies between the balcony and the basin, crossed by a flagstone path edged with Irish moss. Bedding plants in cool pastels are used here for small spaces (*Viola cornuta* and stocks for the winter). Carefully scaled shrubs and small trees (oleanders, pittosporum, citrus, and hibiscus) have all been pruned so that the lines and varied colors of their trunks can be appreciated right at eye level.

Mus has alternated spaces of paving and plantings, low hedges and strong accents, to create a garden of great refinement and sophistication, deliberately keeping a kind of old-fashioned appeal appropriate for the house. As always, he manages an effect of formality without actual symmetry, so that nothing is fixed, the eye keeps moving. Here

Loup de Viane designed this rockery separating house and pool under the spreading shelter of old oak trees. Its subtle mix of forms and foliage colors is particularly well-orchestrated.

intimacy has been created not by an exuberance of floral color but by studied scale and a careful opposition of open and closed spaces, all in greens and whites with just a touch of gray. This is a carefully fashioned jewel of a garden, and a real revelation of what can be done with less than 200 square meters.

A VINEYARD RETREAT

The colorful, jovial, country garden that Mus designed for gastronomic critic Christian Millau and his wife could hardly stand in greater contrast to the city courtyard. By the entrance, citrus balls rise from a tapestry of *Lavandula dentata*, yellow-striped agaves and creeping pale blue plumbago, a composition clearly bearing the Mus signature. The main garden, however, lies between the house and the vineyard, which the Millaus prized as foreground for the blue sheet of the not-far-distant Mediterranean. Here ancient olive trees spring from islands of rampant cistus, rosemary, and lavender, in the heart of a series of paved, pergola-shaded patios set against the house. On the level below, already surrounded by vine rows, is the swimming pool.

The house is linked to the vineyard and pool by low, walled terraces like a series of steps, baking in the sun, and bursting with colorful swaths of flowers for different seasons. Particularly effective are large banks of cassias, whose golden bloom complements the reds and yellows of the vine leaves in the fall. To integrate the vineyard into the garden, moreover, Mus imitated the vintner's common practice of planting a rosebush at the end of every row. Mus has chosen his favorite: the ever-flowering, China rose *odorata* 'Sanguinea'. The courtyard garden in Nice was created around a permanent residence; this one is meant for a vacation home, and had to be both low-maintenance and drought-resistant. It also had to respect the country character of the area, and so Mus has drawn on the palette of traditional Provençal plants. Emerald lawns in the summer, when the surrounding hills turn red-brown, would have been shocking; rather one finds a paved terrace edged with banks of shrubs. Madame Millau, who speaks with great enthusiasm of her garden, considers it to be a lesson in

modesty—in the creation of beauty from a few, simple, well-designed elements.

On the outskirts of the property grow many old-fashioned varieties of peaches, cherries, and almonds. This is a garden for easy living, but also for eating enjoyment. For it is true that intimate gardens often appeal to all five senses: where fragrance envelops; fruits, nuts, vegetables, and herbs intermingle with bloom; sun and shade alternate in just the right dosages; and fountains trickle and murmur in the background. These are pleasure gardens indeed, very much part of a new Riviera *art de vivre*.

The model for this genre was created by Colette, as of 1927, at her celebrated farmhouse, la Treille Muscate, near Saint-Tropez. There the author cultivated five acres of vines, orange trees, fig trees with green and purple fruit, flame-red trumpet vine and wisteria covering the house terrace, and old mimosas with thick trunks. And nearby, the Mediterranean:

"The sea limits, continues, prolongs, ennobles, enchants this piece of land with a luminous shore. . . ." she wrote. Garlic, peppers, and eggplant were immediately planted among the vinerows. Indeed, addressing her garden, she conjured up a vision in which all the senses participate: "I want you adorned, but with vegetable graces. I want you in flower, but not with those tender blossoms which a summer's day, crackling with crickets, turns to ashes. I want you green but not with the inexorable greenery of the palm and the cactus, desolation of a false Africa, Monaco-style. May the arbutus shine next to the orange, and light up that violet fire which spreads over my walls, the bougainvillea. And at their feet, may mint, tarragon and sage raise their heads, high enough so that the hand can easily liberate their perfumes. . . ."

Colette had to abandon her domain when admiring tourists began to invade it, but it still lives in her books. Today's intimate pleasure gardens usually remain as private as possible. Their proliferation may count among the best-kept secrets of the French Riviera. They now exist side by side with the grander variety, which continue to illustrate the better-known, more theatrical part of Côte d'Azur life, and the more spectacular forms of gardening.

In the heart of Nice, small trees pruned at eye level provide ever-changing patterns of light and shade which play against the white villa and an ancient bougainvillea (center).

Amidst lemons and lavender, a Roman emperor looks out over wavy hedging at La Fiorentina toward Villefranche (following pages).

THE SHOW
GOES ON

The legendary gardens of the French Riviera grew up on a grand scale, for the most part setting off palatial houses which were themselves the theater of brilliant receptions. Showcases for their owners' tastes and fortunes, they were often extravagant to a fabulous degree. In pursuit of the ideal décor, many joined Béatrice de Rothschild in defying "the stupid laws of nature and common sense." When Lord Brougham wanted luxurious greenswards around his new villa near Cannes, he saw no difficulty in importing turf from England, by boat, every year. There seemed to be no limit to the prodigious expenditure: Russian nobleman Prince Cherkassky enjoyed variety in the flower beds of his park at La Californie, and every night his forty-eight gardeners were charged with replacing thousands of bedding plants. In this manner, he could be surprised by fresh color upon awaking each morning.

Times, it is frequently said, have changed. Even owners with means rarely resort to such ostentation—and who can imagine employing forty-eight full-time gardeners today? Country domains tucked away in the hills, intimate gardens even in the heart of cities and suburbs—clearly many of today's owners seek more private pleasures.

Nevertheless, the sense of theater and fête have not disappeared from the French Riviera. Many properties still provide décors for the festivities of a dazzling, cosmopolitan society, attracted as much as ever to the Côte d'Azur. Such owners must manage without regiments of caretakers, but they benefit from modern technology. Some gardens designed in the postwar period have had the good luck to remain, if not in the original hands, at least in the care of people able and eager to maintain their original splendor. Not open to the general public and rarely seen in garden publications, these domains have exerted little influence on the Riviera legend as such. Nor can they be principally considered remnants of a brilliant past, since they are flourishing more than ever today. Other grand gardens are recent creations, some just at their beginnings. All of their sites have been exploited for maximum theatricality and dramatic effect, however exclusive the audience may remain. The French Riviera show continues, in the garden world at least. It is still, for a number of privileged owners, magnificent.

As for the laws of nature and common sense, contemporary practice varies. Designers operating on a grand scale may still begin by following novelist Edith Wharton's advice, in her writing on southern gardens, to restructure completely the original site before planting. In other cases, a mountain-top or a terraced hillside may already be sufficiently dramatic, lending itself to the successive unveilings, contrasts of broad prospects, long perspectives and secret spaces which inevitably compose any such garden even today. On the whole, Nature has become more a partner than an opponent, her own histrionic tendencies incorporated and encouraged. So that, although most of these gardens contain intimate and even hidden corners, their overall effect is of an exciting and everchanging show. They remain, above all, spectacular.

A CYPRESS AMPHITHEATER

The Château du Vignal belongs to the Gautier-Vignal family whose descendants took the property in hand in 1970. Its most striking feature is an amphitheater of cypresses, a line circling round the hillside above grassy slopes which replaced the traditional terracing some years ago. The broad valley at the bottom, its whole expanse clearly visible from the entrance gateway, has been filled in with olive trees. Such an original juxtaposition of these two Mediterranean essences is highly dramatic.

Still at the bottom of the hemicycle, but to the right (so as not to block the stage), deciduous trees add the beauty of spring foliage and fall color: two sorts of poplar leafing out at different times, several varieties of oaks, and even the unusual liquidambar.

Inside the gate, the approach road curves round on the left side of the valley, up a slope to the château, which sits behind the grand row of cypresses cutting across the slope, just west of its center. Parts of the building go back to the twelfth century, but most of it was redone with medieval reminiscences in the nineteenth. A particularly lovely paved courtyard with simple elements like box balls in pots is all old Provence. A large, rectangular basin surrounded by a stone balustrade lies just below the house, catching the waters of local springs, a gracious feature in the middle ground; farther out, the cypress towers, linked by an iron balustrade connected to low stone pillars, frame the view of the valley beyond. All along the esplanade on which they stand, glazed terracotta pots add spots of warm, welcoming color to this imposing composition.

A formal staircase about three meters high descends from the middle of the cypress line to the olive tree meadow below, and hides a grotto under its double ramp. The staircase has been covered in the very fine-textured, evergreen climber *Muehlenbeckia complexa*, a gift from the vicomte de Noailles, who made famous use of it around a fountain in his own garden in Grasse. A second, rectangular basin here echoes the larger one on the esplanade above.

A number of inviting paths lead away from the house on several levels to a series of quite different garden rooms, always defined with respect to the large-scaled, curving line of cypresses which dominates the composition. A chapel is smothered with old roses (an early-blooming, cerise-pink climber, followed by the irrepressible 'Mermaid', with 'Golden Wings' on the side). Nearby, stone benches encircle a stone table, the curves enhanced by clipped hedging and box balls. This stately décor is called the Council Chamber. Just beyond, a narrow passage between the cypress curtain and a lavender-covered wall suddenly opens onto the Astronomers' Rendez-vous. Hidden in another corner is an old quarry, where an untamed plane tree with three trunks soars skyward. This is the Sacred Wood, where a mass of violets in early spring hides among mossy stones with strange shapes.

The garden excels in alternating such romantic spaces with strict design, secluded surprises with vast vistas. A formal area

beyond the chapel has been planted with a row of limes, all pruned into parasol shapes, interspersed with four eighteenth-century stone columns and hedged round with tiered greenery: arbutus, Portuguese or Mediterranean tree heather on the sides, laurel hedges behind. A row of box cones and balls leads back to the chapel, for another satisfyingly layered effect. At the east end of the lime trees, an immensely long flight of stone steps leads uphill to the garden's wilder reaches —a copse of magnificent spreading oaks, and a hunting lodge. Another path leads downhill to a charming old ocher-stuccoed farm building, and a series of carved columns.

The strong basic structure of greenery and stonework is highlighted in many places by clumps of echium, or ceanothus, and a wide variety of roses. Indeed, close to the house is a formal rose garden, reached from below through a majestic arch covered with a cascading *Rosa laevigata*. It has been planted on four small terraces for a tiered effect. The lowest retaining wall spills over with an effective mix of catnip, artemisia, and perovskia, all useful for their falling shapes and blue and silver tones. On the level above is a new parterre: four squares of pink and white

At Vignal, the fancifully named Porte de Narbonne leads toward the wilder reaches of the upper garden (above). A double ramp of steps descends below the chapel at Vignal to the tree meadow (below).

Vignal's giant cypresses tower over smaller, secret spaces—some formal, others more romantic (facing page).

A magnificently arched Rosa laevigata invites entry to Vignal's four-tiered rose garden (following page).

groundcover roses enclosed in low, clipped hedges. The central path here leads to a satyr mounted on a pedestal, enjoying the view. Boxwood balls lend strength to the design. Still farther above is a lavender parterre, and on top, groups of echium, ceanothus, datura, and teucrium.

This multileveled rose garden, nestled against the hillside, has a sense of enclosure, but the south side has been left open onto the prospect of the valley beyond. At the back of the uppermost parterre stands an elegant, ocher-colored arch called the Gateway to Narbonne (no doubt in memory of the Roman roads which once spanned the territory from southeast to southwest France).

The steep hillside behind, damaged by

Vignal's esplanade, decked with Anduze jars, looks out through the cypress row toward the meadow below (center).

In spite of its rigor, this is essentially a romantic garden, full of mysterious spaces and discoveries, narrow passages opening suddenly onto breathtaking perspectives—everything on a grand scale. And who could resist the seduction of names like the Astronomers' Rendez-vous?

LA FIORENTINA AND LE CLOS FIORENTINA

Grand gardens generally frame spectacular views of mountains or sea or, ideally, both at once. None more so than the contiguous properties of La Fiorentina and the Clos Fiorentina, perched on the rocky tip of Cap Ferrat. They were largely the creations of designer

fire some years ago, has been newly planted with more than one hundred olive trees. One can circle back above the house through new groves of wilder shrubs, and admire its hidden patios from above.

The garden's outer limits all move gradually into complete wilderness, one of the site's great charms, since both these outskirts and the formal heart have majesty, and share some of the same vegetation (box and arbutus grows wild in these hills). The spaces and shapes are well-designed and proportioned, even in such detailing as the stone steps leading to the greenhouse and work area. Indeed, the stonework is admirable; even the old irrigation canals set in the grass of the meadow are carefully fitted, and beautifully weathered.

Roderick Cameron, author of *The Golden Riviera*, in the decades following World War II. Both today have been lovingly restored and renewed by contemporary owners.

The first to receive Cameron's attention was La Fiorentina. The house, which dates from the first years of World War I, was built by Countess Beauchamp, who engaged Ferdinand Bac to design the three cloister gardens that still exist along the south wall. Cameron's mother, the countess of Kenmare, purchased the property just before World War II. A glamorous Riviera figure of the twenties and thirties, she had first rented La Leopolda, one of Leopold II's many properties in the area, the gardens of which were later redone by Russell Page. But she found this property too formal; living in it, she felt,

The cypress-flanked driveway looks small viewed from the roof of the château (facing page).

would involve too much entertaining. She wanted something less spectacular, and chose La Fiorentina which came accompanied by its smaller and more rustic seventeenth-century *bastide*, the Clos.

She first remodeled the main house at La Fiorentina in imitation of a Palladian villa—a style Cameron describes in his Riviera chronicle as being "half-temple, half-farm. . .the grand and the homespun in just the right quantities." The life led there was not exactly secluded from the world, however; leafing through the visitors' book, Cameron recalls that their intimates after World War II included Louise de Vilmorin, Romain Gary, Somerset Maugham, Freya Stark, Greta Garbo, and the king of Uganda. The property was let at times to renters such as Elizabeth Taylor and Richard Burton. Cameron feared that Miss Taylor might not appreciate the wildlife at La Fiorentina of which he himself was so fond, particularly its giant toads.

Some years later, when his mother was spending most of her time horse racing in Nairobi, Cameron found the main property too expensive to maintain. He sold it and withdrew to the Clos, where he again redesigned the gardens. In the 1970s, he also parted with the smaller property and retired to western Provence, where he then created his last garden, the semi-wild Quatre Sources.

Cameron was a controversial figure, and opinions vary greatly as to the value of his work. British historian Quest-Ritson dismisses him as a mere "garden decorator." But David Hicks, in his book *Garden Design*, considers that "Rory Cameron achieved, for me, total perfection in his garden at Saint-Jean-Cap-Ferrat, with his sure knowledge of texture contrast and scale." There is no doubt, however, that both gardens, although still very private, are spectacular in the true sense of the word.

The site was theatrical to begin with. Wild, tortured Aleppo pines convinced Cameron's mother to buy the property at the outset. The lines around La Fiorentina, the main house and first property to be restored, were already established: formal garden rooms created by clipped hedging nearby, and the country's redolent *maquis* in the distance. Cameron himself describes the first

plantings: the massed, round-leaved bergenias in a great sweep beneath the wind-bent pines; the preference for pale colors and greens, and for odoriferous shrubs such as choisya; the twenty-foot hedges of *Pittosporum tobira* as protection from the east wind; and one of La Fiorentina's most celebrated features, the parterre of orange trees on the esplanade in front of the house. "They were planted four rows deep in lines of ten and the drive swept up the middle. Under the trees we divided the ground up into a geometric pattern of triangles traced in low, clipped box hedges and further delineated, or relieved by alternate spacing of red sand." The trunks and lower limbs were daubed with lime, in imitation of common agricultural practice. Cameron was the first to do this for purely decorative effect, simply "to give luminosity to the dappled, subaqueous light filtering through the dark leaves. I had never seen this done before and we were rather proud of the result."

At La Fiorentina, the pines with their swaths of bergenias, the high hedges along the seafront, and the orange parterres with their diamond hedging and white trunks remain much the same today. Beyond the parterres, a monumental flight of steps leading to the colonnaded house entrance is softened by rows of potted plants on either side.

Scent was ever a constant theme in Cameron's plantings: acacias with their honey fragrance by the gate, *Coronilla glauca* also massed under the pines, *Cestrum nocturnum* by the house, and a lavender parterre underneath the loggia where the family dined in summer (and where a hundred guests can still be fed in elegant comfort). Large pots of lemon and bergamot sat in the corners of this same terrace.

The most famous feature at La Fiorentina, "the great shallow grass steps leading down to the sea," remain much as Cameron described them:

"Falconnet sphinxes frame the stairs and along the descent, on both sides, are planted tapering, twenty-foot cypress. Below these tight, green columns grow dusty clumps of the Canary Islands blue-flowering echium. They advance in waving lines onto the steps, and mixed in with them come small, white flowering convolvulus and the deep-blue Corsican

The oldest and newest parts of La Fiorentina: one of Ferdinand Bac's original cloister-like gardens (center); a newly arranged guest house (above); and a recent, semi-enclosed water garden by the house (facing page).

rosemary. The last, and seventh step is the pool, spilling over into the glittering Mediterranean, and beyond, across Beaulieu Bay, comes the whole dramatic sweep of the mainland piled in a series of precipitous limestone cliffs rising to a height of nearly two thousand feet before collapsing, in folds of varying pastel shades, into Italy."

Cameron kept Ferdinand Bac's three courtyard gardens (one squarish and two long rectangles)

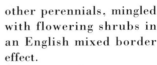

although he does not mention them in his book. Today they still display formal arrangements of clipped greenery and white bloom against the terracotta tones of the ocher walls and earthenware pots. One outside wall has playful crenellations, while the largest of the three gardens has the double arcades and tiled roof of many Mediterranean medieval cloisters.

The gardens at La Fiorentina are given almost entirely to ostentatious display, but there is one stretch of secret garden: an olive walk leading along the east side of the promontory, enclosed by those massive pittosporum hedges, and crossed in the middle by the famous cypress and echium descent to the sea. The olive trees' gnarled trunks are underplanted with swaths of agapanthus and other perennials, mingled with flowering shrubs in an English mixed border effect.

Bac and Cameron notwithstanding, the current owners have felt free to make some major changes: the far end of the house has been extended, still in the Palladian style, and a new courtyard garden has been installed around two fountains spilling over onto a patterned, pebbled *calade* with a long basin beyond. Still very new, this section nonetheless echoes earlier designs. On the wild hillside leading to the Clos, near a chapel where Cameron once liked to retire, a Jacuzzi offers more modern pleasures. A second swimming pool has been added with an elegant pavilion allowing for several additional perspectives on the gardens and the sea view. A former games room in a separate building has become a guest house, and another has been fitted up in the old potting shed. This one looks out onto Cameron's broad lavender parterre, hemmed in by a wonderfully wavy, dark green hedge which in turn sets off another splendid prospect of the bay of Beaulieu.

Potted flowers still provide accents throughout the property, but white-blossomed pelargoniums and impatiens are today seconded by brilliant New Guinea impatiens.

The rust-colored varieties recall Bac's tones; the pale pastels, Cameron's; and the magenta ones provide a note that is entirely modern.

The neighboring Clos Fiorentina, a smaller, more rustic property, always had a different atmosphere. French historians Racine and Boursier-Mougenot emphasize the contrast in orientation and topography of the two gardens: La Fiorentina stands like a lighthouse at the end of the point, its four façades overlooking four different garden sections. The Clos is built into the traditional terraced hillside, facing north. At La Fiorentina, wide paths give access to spaces of great dimension for receptions, whereas at the smaller property, the paths are narrow. At the main house, green rooms lead toward a wilder world of rock and pine; at the

From the gate, steep stone steps lead up from the small road to the house perched above, an ocher-colored *bastide*, the oldest in Cap Ferrat. In front of it, at a right angle to the façade, extends an arched, vine-laden pergola, broad enough to shelter a dining area and frame the familiar but always imposing view of the bay of Beaulieu. On the terraces extending below this sitting space, on both sides, Cameron's formal designs stand out clearly, without fuss. To the west, a small parterre lies beyond the steps mounting from the entrance gate. The main show lies east, however: the original olive tree terraces have been organized into a marvelously subtle and varied display spread out opposite the house pergola like a stage.

La Fiorentina's hydrangea garden is surrounded by citrus and cypress (facing page), while the famous orange trees with whitewashed trunks rise from a diamond-patterned parterre (center).

Clos, echoes of earlier agriculture have been retained. Some of its olive trees are said to be six hundred years old. Unlike other owners on Cap Ferrat, Cameron had the foresight to leave two rows of olive trees along the seafront. He pruned those he kept so that they would frame rather than hide the splendid view.

The Clos suffered a period of serious neglect, but luckily the Moroccan gardener who worked with Cameron has stayed on to the present day. The property now belongs to celebrated couturier Hubert de Givenchy, who clearly appreciates its wonderful balance of open and hidden spaces, of romantic and formal elements. He experiences it as an intimate garden in spite of its elaborate parterres. Certainly, it achieves spectacular effects with much greater simplicity than its neighbor.

Looking from the top to the lowest level of this series of terraces, the eye discovers a series of intricate patterns and juxtapositions, carefully calculated but magic in their effect. At the top, one sees the inviting entrance to an extensive, wisteria-draped pergola, with particularly long and elegant purplish-pink racemes and stone columns. On the next level down stands a row of the original olive trees, still underplanted, as Cameron describes them, with "great cushions of grey-green echium, a handsome contrast to the grey of the olives when they burst out with their blue candle-like flowers in the spring." A narrow, mossy band at their feet is a footpath in acid green. Below this stands a broad, formal rectangle of effulgen aspidistra edged in turn by a row of dark green and spiraling topiary yews.

This is the broadest level of the composition, where gravel-lined spaces and paths surround formally hedged beds. The central path and main visual axis runs beside the spiraling greenery and aspidistra to a tall flight of stone steps beyond, still parallel with the olive trees and their echium banks. Topped by white urns, these stairs lead to the famous mandarin walk, with its white-painted trunks and green globes. "It looks very effective when the lilies are out," wrote Cameron, "their white chalices catching the light filtered through the mandarins' pointed leaves."

At the more intimate Clos Fiorentina, a vine-laden pergola shelters the elegant dining table of Hubert de Givenchy, facing a splendid view of Villefranche (center).

This series of long, parallel levels with its strong contrasts of texture and light is further set off by the billowing greenery of tall

wall, in fact the top part of the pergola on the level below. From here one can again descend to the mandarin walk. Thus the lower parts of the garden, seen in broad panorama from the house terrace, can also be reached through a series of secret spaces. As a result, the property seems much larger than it really is.

Another shaded passage leads through a tunnel under the road toward the saltwater swimming pool, where the olive trees rise above banks of wild grass by the water. On the slopes above, small-scaled terracing has been maintained to set off a box-edged, lavender parterre and the pool pavilion. These spaces are enclosed by tall green hedges and thickets against the back wall, highlighted by

trees separating the Clos from La Fiorentina beyond. The composition cleverly integrates the old terraces, narrow on the hillside, broader as they approach the Mediterranean, where yet another pattern of box-edged gravel paths (rectangles and circles this time) spreads out around a white-trunked persimmon tree.

Another garden entirely has been planned behind the house, sheltered by a steep cliff. Here lies a small topiary parterre, box squares containing tapering box cones, which David Hicks describes as "full of enchantment." Steps with a railing in Chinese Chippendale design lead on to an agapanthus bed, sheltered by tall cypresses. Circling behind the seventeenth-century *bastide*, one descends to the mossy walk with its wisteria

the white trumpets of tree daturas, terracotta pots brimming over with white anthemis, more clumps of arum lilies, and inviting teak benches with plumped-up pillows.

Looking back up the hill from the sea, one has a lovely view of the *bastide* in the top, west corner, with the series of asymmetrical levels in between. All of these effects have been carefully studied, but each appears to be simplicity itself.

Throughout the garden, planting is done in large swaths—the architect's, not the plantsman's solution: the formally massed aspidistra, or naturalized drifts of wild tulips from Greece and Turkey, or dwarf narcissi from the Alpilles. Decoration this may be—certainly it is highly decorative. The Clos Fiorentina, with its play of light on clipped

The Clos's narrow terrace display, from top to bottom, a wisteria pergola, high-pruned olive trees, echium cushions, aspidistra above spiraling yew topiary, and a white-trunked mandarin wa[lk] (facing page).

In a romantic mountain garden, pink rhaphiolepis, deep blue ceanothus, and silvery echium candles highlight a rocky descent toward maritime pines (above).

Many varieties of iris, including this 'Crinolin contribute to the garden's soft colors

Ceanothus 'Delight', backed by oaks and cypresses, rises above formally clipped pittosporum domes and box cones (facing page).

greenery, its falling forms of wisteria and silvery olive foliage in contrast to the strong lines of walls and parterres, remains one of the most beautiful gardens on the French Riviera today.

A HILLTOP RETREAT

How different in style is a large, romantic garden spreading over a wild mountain site (only a few kilometers from one of the backcountry's most popular perched villages) where wave after wave of blossom—shrubs, bulbs, and perennials— flow downward away from the house on a scale few gardeners would dare contemplate. And yet this is largely the work of one woman. The vicomte de Noailles, who sometimes advised her, once said that this was a garden "where everything flowers better than anywhere else."

In the early 1960s, a long, low house was built under the crest of the hill, with windows along the south side to frame the successive blue planes of a spectacular mountain view, the sweep of the descending *maquis* and the blue sea far beyond. The owner's husband did not, at first, want her to garden around the house, except for a rockery to the southwest, and a discreet shrub border opposite the dining room picture windows. The wild landscape was already so dramatic, with its splendid *maquis* vegetation. He had, however, asked Russell Page to embellish it by positioning ten parasol pines east of the house.

But then, in 1969, a fire devastated most of the surrounding woodland. Some copses remain today— rough stands of cork oaks sheltering arbutus and cistus (*salviifolius* and *monspeliensis*). After the initial shock, this disaster proved a blessing in disguise. The trees planted by Page withstood the flames (all but one have grown into majestic specimens). Then the owner patiently began to extend her rockery and her shrubbery into whole rivers of bloom.

She had to deal with a stony plateau about 180 meters above sea level, sloping gently southeast, with granitic soil (mixed with calcareous in spots) only rarely deeper than sixty centimeters. She decided to be guided by the *maquis*, and used largely drought-resistant, evergreen shrubs, whose fragrance she particularly admired. Among the local plants, she especially appreciates tree heathers, filarias (*Phillyrea angustifolia*), spiny broom, wild bulbs such as the orchis 'Serapia', wild asparagus, and terebinths (*Pistacia lentiscus*). She regrets having lost one of the *maquis*'s most characteristic plants, the scrub oak, *Quercus coccifera*, an

excellent truffle variety (truffles once prolif-erated here, but a hungry population during World War II rooted them all out).

In keeping with the Mediterranean cli-mate, she decided to make her garden for the months of April to June (although there are now separate areas for other seasons). She went on to extend the range of the local vege-tation enormously, creating a most unusual and impressive adaptation of Northern gar-den concepts to local conditions.

From English horticulturist Gertrude Jekyll, she took several guiding concepts: the idea of organizing colors into compartments, and of grading their progression through a long border; the importance of keeping sur-prises in store for the garden stroller, whose curiosity must always be stimulated to turn the next corner; the feel of "wild" gardening, which this owner finds most appropriate for her site, where the *maquis* is ever present and the views too vast for any sort of formal foreground.

Another influence was Mien Ruys of the Moer-heim Nurseries in Hol-land, who taught this gardener about leaf tex-ture, lighting effects, space, proportion, and certain color combina-tions. Today she never mixes pale pastels with stronger primaries and thinks of flower col-ors in terms of "yin" and "yang": the former are violet, orange, scarlet, coral, purple, and crimson, while the latter are pastels and grays. She also prefers to use white separate-ly, surrounded by greens; only occasionally does white appear here with pale yellows and true blues. This is not a garden of rare plants, however, since everything must melt into the spreading *maquis*. Rather there is a constant unveiling of masterful blends.

Her early plantings had already proven her talents as a landscaper. To frame the view from the house, unusually magnificent even for this region, she relied on a stretch of lawn edged with a simple, gray-foliaged bor-der in the middle distance—nothing too dis-tracting from the main show. Below this is a group of soft blue floral tones: echiums, bud-dlejas, and ceanothus are underplanted with iris, agathea, and a lavender lantana.

Construction at the rockery began in 1963 using huge granite slabs. It descends toward a pool in one of the old quarries below in a dramatic cascade of ceanothus, cistus (including *C. villosus creticus*), Judas trees, tamarisk, red-foliaged creeping sage, billowy smoke trees, and pale blue-flowering hebes—for a combination of pale yellows, deep reds, pinks, and blues. Some of the few remaining maritime pines in the region pro-vide compelling focal points below. The owner was here advised by Edouard Rosset, former assistant to the world-famous rockery specialist Henri Correvon. Mr. Rosset spent a week in her garden every spring, bringing along many cuttings every time.

The itinerary which now leads below the dining room border meanders across the hill-side from west to east before circling back up behind the house. Each area has its own character: a May garden, for example, is banked with cistus, Chinese peo-nies, *Iris germanica*, blue-flowered flax, soapwort, *Scilla peruviana*, tulips, and nepeta around a care-fully-pruned Judas tree. The scene is backed by purple-leaved berberis, lilacs, and *rugosa* roses.

Then there is a whole hedge of ceanothus 'Delight' (a favorite cultivar); old roses and abelia grouped around an old mill wheel, the round bed outlined with upright stones. Further on is a semicircle of box cones closing off a late summer garden that features lantana spreading around a bench, and more roses underplanted with perovskia. An iris garden laps against a lightning-stunted cypress and the spreading trunks of oak. Still farther on is a veritable river of heathers, contained by rare cistus. Abelias look lovely backed with cotinus, and underplanted with *Amaryllis belladonna*. A plot of medicinal aromatics makes formal use of a stone setting around a tall cypress pil-lar. Here potted sweet geraniums, chrysanthe-mums, dianthus and eriocephalus set off the evergreen herbs, along with the architectural accent of a stooled eucalyptus.

A somewhat formal area has been arranged in the sheltered space in front of the guest house, making striking use of blocks of *Sedum spectabile*. A stone-paved octagon, shaded by two bent parasol pines, is surrounded by a jumble of pastel-colored flowers and shrubs.

So it is that this entire slope, while remain-ing vast, low, and open, contains a panoply of separate spaces. Roderick Cameron admired

*C*lose to the house, in the heart of the mountain garden, gnarled trunks of cork oaks (which survived a great fire in the garden's early days) spread over banks of azaleas planted in special pockets of peat. Elsewhere on this hilltop, the soil is highly alkaline (center and facing page).

how "subtle swirls of colour lap the whitish-gray rocks. Drifts of white and pink cistus and whole rivers of wild thyme are incorporated with sophisticated plants ordered from the English nurseries. The result is most impressive and very pleasing."

In the southeast corner of the slope, a path edged with *Pittosporum tenuifolium* leads through a patch of original woodland to a new garden area, a kind of mock *maquis* using only low-growing, native plants. Indeed, the list of its components reads like a catalogue of the best-loved local resources, though the cultivars are often uncommon: prostrate rosemaries, myrtles, germanders, tree heathers, cistus and laurustinus, thymes and winter savory, dwarf variegated ivy,

small pool. And in a corner, under the shelter of some of the original oaks, is an azalea garden. This unlikely addition to a *garrigue* garden can be grown thanks to special pockets of soil in nylon nets.

Even Eden has its trials and tribulations. This gardener complains of the wild boars, the rabbits, and the magpies which render impossible her dream of a bird sanctuary.

Much as the owner appreciates the evergreen shrubs appropriate for, and often suggested by, her *maquis* setting, she feels every Midi garden should count among its deciduous population roses, irises, and tree peonies. But since each of these plants has periods of unloveliness, they need to be situated in such a way as to provide stunning

bergenias, santolinas, nepetas, junipers and brooms, hyssop, centranthus, oleanders, lavateras, echiums, artichokes, phlomis, coronillas, euphorbias, and mimosa. All are organized in three island beds, placed so as not to block the view. The spectacular squill, *Urginia maritima*, thrives here, surrounded by many shorter cousins: muscari, ornamental garlics, narcissus.

Farther down this slope in another old quarry is the swimming pool, placed here at the suggestion of Russell Page, and protected by a drift of pines and cork oaks pruned to reveal the drama of their trunks.

Close to the house again but on the northeastern side, one discovers the surprise of a Japanese garden designed by a young relative—interesting foliage effects around a

display in season, and stay discreet the rest of the year. This strategy implies a large garden. And this owner works with a vast expanse, which seems even larger because of the variety of different areas encountered along the way, many in one. Each flows into the next with grace and ease, and one wishes never to reach the end.

VISTAS AND VINE LEAVES

All of the preceding gardens have matured over decades, but show gardens continue to be created on today's Riviera. And today, as in earlier times, people with the means to create grand gardens often seek professional advice. So it is that a designer of the stature of Jean Mus often helps clients to create

truly splendid properties. Two of these, the Domaine du Vignal and the Villa Stérenal, both in the backcountry behind Nice, have been much admired for their subtlety and variety, although each has very much its own character.

The Dutch owners of the Domaine du Vignal are greatly interested in local history, proud to own a property that dates back to Roman times and even contains a stretch of Roman road. Known to have been an inn around 1650, later the center of an agricultural domain, it was destroyed at the time of the Revolution. Restored during the nineteenth century, it was renovated again, with Mus's help, about fifteen years ago. Its rural roots have been strengthened and maintained by common accord. So much so that on one occasion, Jean Mus and the owner of the Vignal suddenly found themselves in correctional court together, to defend the construction of a chicken coop built without prior permission from the authorities! They won their case.

This property covers less than four acres. The house, a solidly impressive *bastide* type in soft ocher tones, surmounts a prominence, and the garden spreads around on all four sides.

An avenue of plane trees, reminiscent of those at the stately manor houses near Aix-en-Provence, leads up to the house from an elegant, wrought-iron gate. The avenue, an uncommon feature on the Riviera, concludes at a kind of informal *cour d'honneur*, banked with gray and green santolina on either side of a circular pool and fountain.

This stately, shaded, somewhat enclosed southern approach stands in contrast to the open vistas of the northern slopes. Here the garden design carefully frames two stunning views: a picturesque hilltown to the right, and Grasse rising to the left. At the same time, the design develops a series of interesting planes in the middle ground.

Most impressive is the long sweep of lawn which flows downward, northeast, toward the hilltown. Its movement is slowed and stopped on the horizon by a series of olive trees alternating with cypresses, underplanted with drifts of low shrubbery, the curves broken in just the right places by two towering, spreading oak canopies. The dip of the lawn keeps this elegant edging from blocking the view. Mus's famous use of groundcovers in swaths comes into full play in this composition, which includes clumps of asters, rosemary, and phlomis, islands of agapanthus, terebinths, and germanders (*Teucrium fruticans*), carefully arranged, although not too regularly, for contrasting textures and tones. Different seasons provide spots of color: yellow phlomis in late May, the blue umbels of agapanthus in the summer.

Looking back at the house from the farthest and lowest point of the lawn, one is struck by the broad terrace running along the whole façade of the building above and the impressive staircase which leads down from it. Here, as at La Fiorentina, an irregular line of terracotta pots descending the steps softens their austerity. The façade above is not symmetrical, but ends to the east in a large archway. This great curve, clearly visible from afar, is repeated in the forms of the shrubbery below the house to the east of

the staircase, where pruned and unpruned cypresses also repeat the verticals of chimneys on the roof above.

The balustrade of the terrace running along the house is punctuated with the points of yew cones—but one must be actually up on the terrace itself to realize that these form part of a formal, Italianate rectangle, at the far end of which presides a statue of the god of love! He stands, backed by a cypress curtain, and framed by the low, billowing forms of rhaphiolepis, with the patterns and soft tones of old rust-colored terracotta tiles in the foreground.

Below the house, at the northwestern corner, lies the swimming pool, surrounded by spiky fountains of phormiums with their yellow, lime-green, and rusty tones (nothing bright). Dark *Grevillea rosmarinifolia*; the deep, winy foliage of berberis; strong fans of aloes; and, of course, palm trees make this an exotic island in predominantly yellow-green tones, held together by the rust-colored terracotta tiles around the pool. There is no abrupt transition between this and the lawn spreading to the east: the link is provided by a big bed of velvety blue-flowered perovskias mixed with the somewhat exotic shapes of nandinas under a large olive tree, echoing those which border the grassy dip further on.

A small patio on the second storey of the house, also at its northwest corner, looks toward Grasse. This view has been beautifully framed by successive planes of vegetation, one of the happiest plantings on the entire Riviera. In the foreground, on either side of the steps leading from this patio down to the pool, two large, earthenware jars on slightly different levels contain boxwood balls. Just outside, twin dwarf fan palms, one higher than the other, lead the eye beyond. Still further down, an alternating series of ceanothus, dwarf pittosporum, and Corsican rosemary mingle with yellow-flowered phlomis to fill the middle part of the picture. Below, the arching, feathery crowns of sumac, holding up their velvety red candles much of the year, are punctuated by cypress pillars, and contrast with the somewhat larger, silvery, rolling forms of a Russian olive (*Eleagnus angustifolia*). All of these subtly-blended textures help create a series of planes of ever taller vegetation as the slope declines. They provide a rich but discreet foreground for the rising geometries of the medieval city in the far distance.

Le Vignal's most famous feature, however, lies along the west side of the house, extending below the formal approach area. This is the Provençal Garden, a series of lavender waves, each lapping the foot of an ancient olive tree. The rhythms of this quite simple, totally Mediterranean planting are truly spectacular when the lavender is in flower (*Lavandula vera*). But even during the rest of the year, the shapes and scale make for a very satisfying picture—one that appeared for some time, in fact, on the menu of Roger Vergé's fashionable restaurant, le Moulin de Mougins!

Much else has gone into the making of this garden: clever but hidden drainage ditches bordering carefully-graded slopes; a discreet tennis court, a vegetable garden and even a small vineyard; a charming caretaker's house

On the other side of the Domaine du Vignal, a formal avenue of plane trees (rare in Riviera gardens) joins the wrought-iron entry gate to the cour d'honneur. The rounded box cones are a typical Jean Mus accent.

next to an ancient winecellar; a much photographed seventeenth-century fountain with a satyr's head, presiding over the passage back up to the north courtyard. The owners quite deliberately maintain the customs of southern landed gentry, respecting the original agricultural vocation of the land. Vine leaves have been incorporated into the motifs of the wrought-iron entry gate, recalling the name and former raison d'être of the property.

EXOTIC EXPLORATIONS

A much larger property designed by Jean Mus, the Villa Stérenal, lies in the seclusion of wooded hills near Saint-Paul-de-Vence. Here the owners and designer have together

Olive crowns and carefully outlined black trunks rising from drifts of lavender are practically a signature planting of Jean Mus, here at the Villa Stérenal.

low, spreading groundcovers, from which emerge the red-tinged trunks of *Washingtonia* and date palms, and pines with similar parasol shapes. These serve to frame a *buffet d'eau* in the far distance, a rock-lined pond at its foot.

To the east, an exotic garden surrounds the swimming pool with summer-flowering plants—agapanthus, hibiscus, lantana, and fragrant mandevilla. Behind, a series of small walks and pergolas lead to other, more recently designed garden areas beyond, including a whole village of guest houses and service buildings.

The transitions between these three areas, smaller wedges farther from the house, are not immediately visible, and contain more

created a whole park full of different gardens on ten acres.

A modern house sits at the center of a fan-shaped spread, divided into three wedges, each with a different character, but all visible from the house terrace.

To the west, the Italian Garden: a formal walkway leads under a series of pergolas supporting wisteria and jasmine draped over an elegant pool. Marble steps flanked by cypress columns and massed olive trees and citrus lead upward to a pink, marble-faced garden pavilion above, rising imposingly like an Italian stage décor.

To the south, the English Garden: two marble lions guard the entrance to an ocean of heathers (some 5000 plants of *Erica darleyensis*), mixed with nandinas and other

secret garden spaces. The most imposing is a shaded, sunken green circle of pines and pittosporums, a kind of green theater where outdoor concerts are held. Impressive carved urns stand guard at its entrance.

On the outskirts, more and more garden areas keep appearing for further walks: one, alongside a hedge of mixed, red- and yellow-berried pyracantha leads to a greenhouse half-shaded by tumbling wisteria. Elsewhere, another wooded area has been cleared of its undergrowth to make a croquet lawn. The distant part of the hilltop is in fact an old Ligurian encampment, and large sections of its walls have been uncovered and restored, then allowed to develop a natural carpet of pine needles. A rustic garden pavilion sits here, its approaches banked with azaleas, brilliant spring accents in the dappled light. Most ambitious perhaps is the mock-ruined tower of recent construction which stands hidden at the center of a yew labyrinth. The white limestone of the area allows both the restoration of old walls and the creation of new "antiquities" without glaring discrepancies in the stonework. Finally, the newest garden is a lavender parterre designed around citrus globes on several shallow terraces, linked by a central pergola soon to be smothered in old varieties of rambling roses.

This stupendous complexity was achieved in less than six years, starting from impenetrable woodland. Jean Mus has found full scope here for several of his favorite types of garden design: infinite variations in different parts of

side with subtropical. Mus makes the most of these unique possibilities. Rather than keeping each plant type in its separate category he thinks of actual volumes, textures, and colors apart from conventional associations.

In a garden of this size, Mus can also play with his beloved double perspectives: the wall of water is a focal point from the house, but one can also walk through a series of garden pictures to reach it, and from it look back toward the house. The plantings are designed for effective framing in both directions.

To create such a garden in such a short time takes not only vision and imagination, but also tremendous organization. Clearing the forest, redesigning the terrain, installing automatic watering and fire protection, con-

Besides classic mixtures at the Villa Stérenal, Mus also dares to set palms amidst purple heather (Erica darleyensis) and nandina (center).

the garden on the theme of massed, contrasting groundcovers at the foot of trees, for example. He has allowed some daring juxtapositions: heathers with palm trees is a shocking combination if one thinks only in terms of common connotations. But in February, purple swaths beautifully set off the red-tinged trunks of a carefully spaced row of palms, while the middle distance is mediated by the feathery bamboo-like clumps of nandina whose red berries, at that time of year, pick up and reinforce the color scheme. Other seasons must be kept in mind, however, and each will have its own tonalities—swaths of early-summer lavender will also set off the palms. This is a region where north meets south, the Provençal backcountry meets the Mediterranean, temperate vegetation thrives side by

structing new garden walls and outbuildings or incorporating existing ones—all of these activities mean coordinating many different types of workmen before planting even begins. But even when the garden is in place, the job is still not done. Mus's striking masses of evergreens require a particular "soft" pruning technique that few gardeners have acquired on their own, so that training personnel for future upkeep is a large part of his task.

The drama of such a garden from the first glorious sweep of the eye across the three different parts visible from the house terrace, through the spectacle gradually unfolding in the outlying areas, must first exist in the mind of a master director, much as for a moviemaker. The result is a grand showcase garden indeed.

LE DOMAINE DU RAYOL

Creating or restoring an ambitious garden is difficult enough when one person—owner or landscaper—is in charge. How much harder with those fabulous properties which belong to the public domain or to associations, where each decision must be ratified by several different bodies. And yet, the future of show gardens on the French Riviera may lie more and more in their value as spectacle for an increasingly discerning audience—the public at large. The municipalities of both Menton and Hyères have assumed great responsibilities for properties in their charge. Some spectacular gardens were of course designed for public use from the start: the Exotic Gardens in Monaco, founded by Prince Albert I in 1897, now claim to receive more than 500,000 visitors a year. The beautiful cactus garden at the village summit in Eze, though much smaller, is a strong competitor.

The picturesque coast near Hyères, between Le Lavandou and Saint-Tropez, contains a number of splendid properties in spite of precipitous real estate development in recent years. Three of these have had the good fortune to fall under the protection of an association called the Conservatoire du Littoral. One, the Domaine du Rayol, is on its way to becoming one of the Riviera's most picturesque gardens. Celebrated landscaper Gilles Clément has been engaged to redesign this wild valley opening onto a sandy beach between two rocky promontories.

The Domaine du Rayol has had a rich, typically Côte d'Azur history. Before World War I, a banker, Alfred Théodore Courmes, created a hideaway here for his young wife on forty-four acres of land. An Art Nouveau house was built in 1910: sylphs still play the flute on its cream-colored façade. In 1925, the owners moved to an Art Deco villa elsewhere on the property.

In 1934, crushed by gambling debts in Monaco, Courmes threw himself into the sea. In 1940, aeronautics pioneer Henry Potez settled at the Domaine, hired twenty gardeners, designed an orchard, planted terraces full of exotic trees: carobs, bitter oranges, and palms. As his passion grew, even in those difficult times, so did the garden, to which he added four hundred species, mainly from the southern hemisphere.

A period of decline followed, but the current caretaker, Henri Robinia, and Etienne Gola, mayor of Rayol and former overseer on the property, spared no effort in trying to maintain it throughout its period of adversity. Now it is destined to become not only one of the most original gardens of the region, but also a center for garden study.

The Conservatoire du Littoral purchased the property in 1989. Clément is now creating a most imaginative park here, with the help of botanist François Macquart-Moulin and the faithful Henri Robinia. Twelve acres will be maintained as gardens, where the public, accompanied by trained botanists, will be able to discover both the wild flora of the local *maquis*, and the superb collections.

Gilles Clément is celebrated for his conception of the *jardin en mouvement*, in which all human intervention is guided by the spontaneous tendencies of the vegetation. His work respects plants, the spirit of place, and historical reference, but at the same time provides a dynamic conception of flux and evolution. Since this garden is botanical and pedagogical as well as horticultural, plant families will be kept together—a challenge in garden design.

A certain number of precious plants remain from earlier stages (as do the buildings and the pergola). These include Australian mimosas, bottle brushes and eucalyptus; Chinese persimmons and Mexican cacti; one *Araucaria imbricata*; and of course the local parasol and Aleppo pines and cork oaks.

The restoration of each space procedes slowly, taking into account not only the garden's organization by geographical zones but soil quality, watering possibilities, general perspectives, textural contrasts—everything which goes into good garden design on a grand scale.

Starting off from the gatehouse in the southwest corner of the huge amphitheater, one moves upward along a pittosporum hedge (which is high enough to hide the view), past an enormous, picturesque eucalyptus whose fallen strips of bark have been prettily arranged at its feet, to emerge, suddenly, onto the brilliant South African garden. This extends at the foot of a long, high pergola. Agaves mix with purple-blooming polygala,

The Roman-inspired pergola at Rayol, its squared wooden beams set on stone pillars, dates from the 1920s. Underneath lies a three-toned mosaic which Clément himself made from beach pebbles and weathered bits of broken glass.

orange leonotis, banana trees, and others in a grand splash of color. Once galtonias had sown themselves all through this plantation, but an inexperienced gardener dug them all up by mistake—a small example of the mishaps of properties administered by groups, societies, and public bodies. But the team at work today is determined and knowledgeable.

The pergola rising above the South African garden dominates the entire valley in one grand sweep that allows the viewer to take the measure of the garden's scope as it reaches toward the sea. Broad steps originating still higher on the slope above descend under the pergola's beams, continuing straight down the steep hillside where they are edged by towering cypresses, one of the longest examples of a strong vertical axis in any Riviera garden. Clément has carefully massed trees and shrubs on the opposite, somewhat lower incline to incite the eye to move upward. If one walks round the valley to this far slope, one discovers a wonderful viewpoint back on the pergola and its long staircase. Still looking back, the eye is drawn to the very top of the hill, above the pergola, toward another magnificent eucalyptus.

The spaces on either side of this upper path, above the pergola on the garden's north rim, have been planted with a zoysia lawn, and surrounded by Australian plants, especially callistemons and grevilleas. From here, a discreet lateral path leads east along the curve of the hillside to a giant rockery, where huge slabs of golden stone have been brought from the quarries at Bormes-les-

Mimosas to make raised beds for a variety of yuccas and cacti. Here are more southern hemisphere rarities: two varieties of grass trees (*Xanthorrhoea*). Their stocky trunks are regularly burned and blackened in grass fires in their native southwestern Australia.

From this exotic display, the road circles round to the more serene seclusion of the old farmhouse. Other low retaining walls layer the slope above the road in a simple, beautiful rhythm, a space which will be left open in a garden so full of large trees and woodland copses elsewhere.

Below the road, a ravine has been carpeted with white-flowering periwinkle and banks of acanthus. Clément will add here a river of arum lilies and other bulbs, the whole backed by mature stands of multitrunked cork oaks. This is the site chosen for special experimentation with the *jardin en mouvement*, intermingling spontaneous, natural evolution with gentle control.

In the hollow below, one can see a small bridge and a cascade, the heart of the Oriental Garden that is reached after several more turns. Above the drive extends wild *maquis* vegetation, natural to the area. The path now slopes around to the viewpoint back toward the pergola, and then beyond to the 1930s Potez villa with its formal, brick-edged, Art Deco parterre.

From there it is a short distance to the beach, with stunning sea views both up and down the coast, where wind-bent pines above tumbling rocks shelter beautiful local wild plants in masses, such as the protected, silvery Jupiter's beard (*Anthyllis barba-jovis*)

The farm buildings at Rayol will eventually house a nursery selling cuttings and seeds from the foundation's collections. Just beyond will be an open space for playing boules, the popular southern lawn bowls game.

and asphodels. The fishing of sea urchins is forbidden in this bay, leaving undisturbed a site which will later on house a marine garden, partly underwater.

Circling back toward the garden's center, one arrives at the bottom of the hillside steps in the heart of the valley. To the east, a whole slope has been planted with variegated, silvery-blue and red-leaved grasses (*Carex*) in a beautiful tapestry effect. A ravine shelters the New Zealand Garden, where huge fountains of thick-leaved, all-green phormiums intermingle with giant tree ferns. The Oriental Garden also lies along this path.

The slope west of the cypress staircase will be devoted to plants from the Americas, and already sports tall clumps of *Washingtonia* palms, a variety of tender sages, and nolinas. The stone steps will be further extended by a callistemon avenue. Elsewhere are planned a lotus basin, a cistus perspective, and the Planisphere terrace with its garden of artemisias (examples of this species exist on all five continents). There will be an Asiatic collection of cycads and persimmons, a meadow of Mediterranean wildflowers (annuals and perennials), a section for coastal plants of the inland sea, a pelargonium walk including agapanthus and eucalyptus, a nasturtium walk among feijoas, and other promenades devoted to daturas and phormiums.

Southern hemisphere plants will provide the domain's main theme, along with collections from all around the Mediterranean and the marine underwater garden. A bookstore is planned in a new building at the entrance. The Centre de Formation des Jardins du Monde Méditerranéen will be housed in the original Art Nouveau building, which is now the gatehouse.

Such ambitious plans take courage and patience and Le Domaine du Rayol is still just in its beginnings. Help has been enlisted from botanists at the Villa Thuret and lecturers from the center for garden design at La Napoule. But the Domaine is already a magic place even for the uninitiated, a treasure trove for the knowledgeable.

TORRE CLEMENTINA

Some Belle Epoque follies have fallen into the hands of adventuresome, private owners with the means to create new gardens from the ruins of the past with the same panache as their earlier counterparts. Such is the fate of the Torre Clementina, set on a wild hillside on Cap Martin where the princes of Monaco once took their hunting parties, and where, later on, realtors developed an enclave so elegant that Princess Eugenia elected to have a residence there. The Torre Clementina was first designed after 1900 for Ernesta Stern, *femme de lettres* and hostess of renown, who received the worldly and artistic elites of her time. Not content with contemporary celebrities, she resorted to seances to convoke Napoleon as well, and it is said he did not disdain the rendez-vous. Historians Racine and Boursier-Mougenot quote Ferdinand Bac's colorful portrait of this eccentric lady, who liked "grandeur and power as they existed

Echium and felicia on this level (above), white anthemis below (center), flank winding garden paths leading from one architectural fragment to another.

The Torre Clementina on Cap Martin was originally built in styles ranging from Byzantine to Roman to pure fancy. Today's restoration includes intricately patterned mosaics below the house (facing page).

through the ages, and who draped her massive, pale form with Merovingian pendants."

Ernesta Stern commissioned architect Lucien Hesse to build a romantic fortress with both turrets and loggia, which still stands in much its original form today. An even more important contributor was Raffaele Maïnella, who designed both the interiors and the garden. A painter and, it is said, former hairstylist, he took delight in combining as many periods, styles, and building materials as he could imagine—brick, stone, translucid onyx panels, and pebble mosaics all intermingle. Bac wrote of the result that "China and Japan, Syracuse and Trebizond, the translucid marbles of San Miniato compete for attention in their zeal to decorate this dwelling and render it mysterious, in an accumulation of effects which lack only the Christian sense of moderation."

In other words, the Torre Clementina was yet another of those great surrealistic mosaics—collections of travel memories and cultural fragments—so typical of the French Riviera just after 1900. The park laid out on the steep slope from the road above to the sea below was conceived in the same spirit, while a courtyard area above the road contained a Japanese garden and a miniature Greek

theater. To the right of the house, a strong axis between giant cypresses extended straight down the hillside, imposing and impressive in its somewhat gratuitous majesty. It is now being replanted.

The Torre Clementina has been in a turmoil of restoration since 1985, entrusted to the Boston firm of Charles T. Young (John Bolt being the architect in charge). Landscape architect Robert Truskowski, from Laguna, California, began redesigning the gardens in 1987. The grand old cosmopolitan spirit lives again—indeed, one of Mr. Truskowski's other clients is Mick Jagger. The designer works on properties from Austria to the Antilles, and feels that the climate of Cap Martin is very similar to his home territory in California.

The main part of the garden, the lines of which are still evident, is a curving path meandering from the lower reaches of the house from viewpoint to viewpoint, down to the rocky stretches sheltering the beach below. At regular intervals stand garden kiosks, medieval and Byzantine sculpture and fountains, all in much the same style as the house—here a Romanesque column, there a set of brick and stone arches, elsewhere a baroque grotto. These are revealed one after the other on the descent, which

Torre Clementina's newly installed pool has been built with underwater windows, providing a glimpse in from paths below the house (following pages).

remains a kind of romantic unveiling of successive treasures.

A strong framework is provided by the cliff itself and a series of particularly magnificent parasol pines, which tower above the architecture and frame the sea view of Monaco with appropriate grandeur. These giant trees anchor the man-made folly, in all its manifold incarnations, to the landscape.

House and garden have now been linked in a series of original and spectacular connections. A swimming pool now juts out like a tongue at the foot of the fortress, its lines softened by a pergola draped with 'Black Dragon' wisteria. A series of brick and stone arches echo Maïnella's style in their inner recesses, half open, half closed, and shelter a large round basin which is, in fact, a Jacuzzi, giving onto the pool and the sea view beyond. Arcades and niches with statues and colonnades connect a labyrinthine series of changing rooms and a bar.

But the most amazing effects lie on the garden descent below. Along the east side of the building, a series of square, paved landings have been banked with masses of polygala and other shrubby groundcovers, connecting the house to the meandering promenade. Before reaching the latter, however, one passes again at the foot of the house, through another semicircular colonnade which frames the sea view on its outer edge. Looking inward, one discovers through a thick, glass panel the depths of the swimming pool, like an enormous aquarium whose inhabitants are the swimmers. The latter, in turn, if they dive deep, will face the garden and the view of Monaco through the colonnade, from under water. A small canal runs at the foot of the columns, making a playful aquatic connection.

All down the hillside, stone, brick, marble, and pebble constructions extend the house into the garden. Every detail has been carefully considered, and these different materials are interwoven with great ingenuity: in one case, architect Bolt designed a new mosaic floor in three different colored stones which had to be perfectly calibrated for the desired effect. Carved balustrades like those by the house outline the garden path and surround the viewpoints where, by great good luck, some of the original structures with

their beautiful, aged patina still stand. They were discovered in a jungle of pittosporum gone so wild that, when the landscapers first began to work here, the sea view was completely blocked.

The gardens have already taken shape. Mr. Truskowski imagined them as a broad tapestry, with broad strokes using color and texture in mass. Within is a series of garden rooms around focal points. Plantings have been layered to provide shelter and privacy. For example, a collection of rare camellias has its own, special atmosphere near at hand, but from a distance it is viewed as a bold splash in the overall composition. Everywhere plantings are thus detailed for close examination, but meant also to be viewed as part of a grand sweep.

In one place, tall oleanders and pittosporums have been pruned as multi-trunked trees amidst swaths of agapanthus and mondo grass. Yuccas and dwarf fan palms serve as special accents and at one turning in the path, a small stretch of lawn under more pine canopies has been backed by ever-higher layers of cycads and palms. In the lower garden, one suddenly comes upon another marvel: a recent imitation of the ruined Moorish pergola which Maïnella built for the nearby Villa Cypris, and which the present owner of the Torre Clementina wished to have in his own garden.

So it is that the grand Riviera spirit still lives on in the private domain of Cap Martin. Extravagance and daring combine once more in an adventure which involves even more innovation than restoration.

LA CASELLA

La Casella is probably the most widely-acclaimed garden of recent years—begun only in 1985! In this short time, its owners, Klaus Scheinert and Tom Parr, have realized an elegant and sophisticated synthesis of all the Riviera's best elements: Provençal, Italian, English, and purely personal.

The house already sets the tone: designed in 1960 by Robert Streitz, a pupil of Emilio Terry, its form was inspired by the pavilion designed by the architect Gabriel for Madame de Pompadour at Fontainebleau; its soft, warm colors by Neapolitan models. Tom Parr, chairman of the well-known decorating

firm of Colefax and Fowler, renovated and decorated it and began work on the garden, creating the original, sheltered courtyard to the east. Then Klaus Scheinert, who had never gardened before, began to take an interest. It is largely through his efforts that La Casella has become one of the great, contemporary showcase gardens of the Riviera.

Scheinert began by visiting famous properties to find out what would grow well on similar sites, and was particularly inspired by La Mortola, the Villa Noailles, and the Chèvre d'Or. He feels it may have been an advantage to start off without preconceived notions brought from another climate. Indeed he began with a baptism of ice—1985 was a year of killer frosts. The west terraces, formerly a jasmine and bitter orange plantation, had already lost almost everything in the similarly disastrous year 1956. So, for better or for worse, there was a clean slate.

At La Casella, Plumbago capensis *spills out of an Anduze jar (center). Lemon balls rise out of box squares near pots of agapanthus, rows of lavender, and 'Iceberg' roses (below).*

The decision to use only plants that grow well locally was surely a wise one, and not a limitation in a region that can support such a wide variety. The design of La Casella makes full use of the available range by mixing Italian perspectives among clipped greenery with English floral display.

Both owners belong to the persuasion of pastel colors, feeling that summer gardens in the south should be essentially green. The typical Mediterranean blend of cypress, box, laurel, and olive is enriched by the Côte d'Azur addition of citrus foliage, vibrant and fresh all year round. In this setting, the cool pastels chosen for the floral décor contrast beautifully with the warm, subtle variations of the ocher-colored house. Bright flowers are admitted indoors for gay country bouquets, but these grow in the cutting garden (sweet William and striped tulips for the early season, sunflowers, green zinnias, cosmos, and pinks later on).

But even if this garden is at its best in spring and fall, summer is not without bloom: found at a level above the house is a glorious rectangle of blue agapanthus, with citrus pillars and stone obelisks in the center. And one long, lower terrace to the west is edged with a formal pattern of Iceberg roses and lavender, a beautiful blend. On the patios, however, only the most discrete pelargoniums are allowed.

Fragrant pelargoniums in tiered pots are indeed the first display to greet the visitor by the house's eastern façade, under the filtered shade of ancient olive trees.

La Casella's myrtle walk and the pergola above can be glimpsed from the house, past a clump of Convolvulus cneorum *(facing page).*

*L*a Casella
has several outdoor
sitting and dining
rooms, for enjoyment at
different times of the
day (above). Even the
caretaker's house invites
repose under the long,
perfumed racemes of a
Wisteria floribunda
'Alba' (facing page).

From this departure point, the garden unfolds, act after act, scene after scene—for like all grand gardens, La Casella is many in one.

Parr's original, sunken courtyard to the southeast, sheltered by dusky hedges, has elegantly patterned paving spreading out like sunrays in homage to an unusual familiar spirit: a sculpted elephant spurting plumes of water. Large terracotta pots present powder-blue plumbagos trained over arched supports; exotic *Durantas* (sometimes called Golden Dewdrop), whose blue flowers and orange fruit appear at the same time; *Murrayas* with their fragrant foliage and repeat flowering; *Sparmannia africana*; *Iochromas*; and perfumed tuberoses.

South of the house lies a sheltered sitting area while the main part of the garden, a series of narrow terraces on the steep hillside, stretches to the west. Cypresses and olive trees both frame and hide transitions, so that one is ever drawn on toward intriguing perspectives.

Visible—and strikingly beautiful—from the southern sitting terrace is the blue and white garden, the first part to be planted. It mixes dimorphothecas, white-flowered hebes, eryngiums, violets, allogynes, plumbagos and ceratostigmas, 'Victoria' sages, convolvulus, and even aubrietas in a tapestry which keeps its interest year round. Pale pink Japanese anemones have also been allowed to infiltrate.

Glimpsed, too, from the house terrace is the highly elegant myrtle walk; a formal promenade of fine-textured lawn; and a high wall covered by a whole succession of different climbers clipped in fans close to the wall:

mandevilla and *Holboellia latifolia* with heavenly scents, pink bignonias, and white solanums. At one point they surround a carved stone fountain, and further along, a stone bench outlined in trimmed box. Glazed urns on pedestals punctuate the long wall.

Looking back at the house, one finds it framed by tall towers of laurel, rising like a fortified gateway above which the peaks and domes of cypress and olive trees stand in contrast. Spires of blue echium complete this strong composition.

On the broad terrace above the myrtle walk, a dramatic pergola made of brick and stone columns linking wooden beams has been planted with exuberant climbers allowed to trail and ramble, including the lovely 'Black Dragon' Chinese wisteria. The pergola stands between twin, two-toned santolina parterres at either end: raised, square beds around Anduze jars.

Along the outer edge of this terrace, pots of plumbago provide color for a later season. Along the back wall, low box teepees are interplanted with the starry, white bloom of low-growing *Jaborosa integrifolia*. One can climb above, amidst a spill of exotic plants around another fountain with sculpted lions' heads, for another look at this splendid composition.

These spaces, with their strong design and rich texture, are already spectacular. But the showiest part of the garden remains its western descent, where an ingenious succession of patterns and tones reflects continuing experimentation with focal points and their framing. The terraces on this west side

Hidden
below the house at La
Casella, a quiet strip
of lawn is backed by
formal hedging (center).
Each of the western
terraces has its own
composition, its
alternance of views and
enclosure (facing page).

of the property are smaller and narrower than those close to the house, and are reached by a flight of stone steps running up and down the hillside. Viewed from this descent, each is a stage in itself, to be entered and explored. Some have been planted to accentuate their length, others cut up into smaller compartments. And since hidden connections link the levels at their far ends as well, a kind of zigzag itinerary becomes possible, so that no vantage point may be missed. The outer-edge plantings of each terrace provide backdrops for those below, and views up and down are as carefully planned as those along each level.

In one instance, the focal point is pruned oak balls surrounding a bench, their shapes echoed by two stone balls at the terrace entrance. Its length is accentuated by rows of lavender along the outer edge (spilling over to form part of the décor below). Against the back wall, more lavender mingles with the velvety blue of perovskia and more echium spikes.

In contrast to these long lines, another terrace has been broken up into a checkerboard mix of shrubs and perennials, its paths outlined in santolina: here ceanothus (there are ten different varieties at La Casella), *Solanum rantonnettii*, *Bupleurum*, the white poppy *Romneya coulteri*, and others shrubs not exceeding three meters in height are set off by tall laurel cones.

Below this series of formal gardens are a fruit orchard, a vegetable plot, and the caretaker's cottage. Finally, at the bottom of the property, near the driveway which circles back up the hill, is the English Garden, an informal shrubbery in yellows, whites, and blues, which contains more solanums, abutilons, phlomis, acanthus, the yellow, flax-flowered *Reinwardtia indica*, *Fremontodendron*, senecios, wild daturas, melianthus, lavateras, tree peonies, Japanese anemones, and polygonums among musk and climbing roses, blue and white iris, columbines and "Burmese" day lilies. A massive, dark green hedge wall rises behind and anchors this profusion, its top sculpted into a low-relief lintel for a strongly architectural effect. Along the driveway opposite, a row of glazed, terracotta jars presents a formal array of white agapanthus flanked by balls of green santolina.

This garden is in constant evolution, but in the few years of its existence, it has achieved real stature—and acquired several hundred different species and varieties of plants. Above all, the domain displays a definite personal style: a love of pattern and design on the grand scale, but also a sensitivity to detail and texture. The wealth of plants is set off by an equally rich range of mineral elements in the pavings and sculptural décor. This is a garden made to be seen, but also very much a garden to watch.

Indeed, northwest of Nice, among those mellow hills where terraced fields of roses for the perfume industry still overlook wild, wooded valleys, many contemporary gardeners look to La Casella for inspiration.

Landscaper Jean Mus considers that there are two main tendencies in the gardens of the French Riviera today. On the one hand, those which are personal follies, whose limits are set only by their owners' individual fancy. Many collectors, both great and small, have pursued exoticism in this spirit of making dreams come true, as much as from scientific curiosity. The best-known extravagances were created right on the coast—not just a few famous examples but literally by the dozen, for about a century. The Scotsman's Gothic castle called Smith's Folly and the pleasure garden of fin de siècle writer Maurice Maeterlinck are still near neighbors on the road east of Nice. Such creations represent an extraordinary heritage for any region to absorb, a unique phenomenon in Europe and perhaps in the world.

The second tendency Mus observes is the Riviera garden conscious of its Mediterranean roots, which becomes a concentration of the traditional landscape (both wild and agricultural). It has grown up largely in the backcountry. Its lines are strong, its conception sober although often grandiose in the Italian manner. Influential landscape architects in the region, from Harold Peto to Russell Page, have often preferred this style, and Jean Mus does as well.

Today, it might be said that owners of grand gardens often combine the two tendencies. If rustic refinement has now become the fashionable theme, its realizations, in their infinite variety, set the stage for ever more fanciful dreams.

Queen
Victoria called the
French Riviera "this
paradise of nature."
The wild seaside
gardens of famous
couturière Madame
Carven prove this is still
true today (following
page).

ADDRESSES FOR GARDEN LOVERS

The French Riviera possesses an extremely rich concentration of parks and gardens, historical and contemporary, for each successive season of its ever-unfolding show. Many of these are open to the public, but only those described in this book are listed here. Information on others can be found in the bibliography at the end of this book. Since opening hours and conditions vary from season to season and year to year, it is best to telephone ahead for exact information.

These great gardens serve as models and sources of inspiration both to the growing number of nurseries providing an ever wider ‚range of adapted plants, and to the hundreds of landscape gardeners, professionally trained or self-taught, now working on the Riviera. At the same time the swelling ranks of Riviera gardeners look more and more for decorative objects, especially pottery. This entire dimension of the Riviera gardening is expanding day by day. (The page numbers in parentheses refer to the photographs in the book).

GARDENS OPEN TO THE PUBLIC:

BONSAI ARBORETUM
Camaret 84850, Chemin du Val de Pôe, Biot 06410. Tel. 04 93 65 63 99. Fax. 04 93 65 10 78 99.
Next to the Musée Ferdinand Léger.

CHÂTEAU DE GOURDON
Gourdon 06620. Tel. 04 93 09 68 02.
A private property belonging to Mr. and Mrs. Glachon. But the garden is open to the public depending on the season. A striking mountain castle with a series of hanging courtyards and gardens, which go back to the seventeenth century, also includes a herb garden designed by Loup de Viane in 1972.

CHÂTEAU DE LA NAPOULE
(Director: M. A. Janet)
Avenue Henry-Clews, Mandelieu-La Napoule 06210. Tel. 04 93 49 95 05. Fax. 04 92 97 62 41.
Henry Clews, an American sculptor, and his wife, Mary, had this medieval castle rebuilt at the beginning of the century.

CHÂTEAU DU VIGNAL
Monsieur and Madame Gautier-Vignal
Contes, Nice 06390.
Tel. 04 93 79 00 11. Fax. 04 93 79 19 90.
Open only to small groups and upon written request. Tastings of the prize-winning olive oil produced on the grounds are available. (p.151, 152,156,172,173).

CLOS DU PEYRONNET
(Owner: William Waterfield)
Av. Aristide Briand, Menton 06500.

Tel. 04 93 35 72 15. Fax. 04 93 35 72 25.
Open only to small groups upon booking. A very beautiful exotic garden and a world famous collection of bulbous plants. The same family has lived here for three generations. (p. 55, 56, 60, 67).

DOMAINE DE RAYOL
(Owner: Le Conservatoire du littoral)
Avenue du Commandant-Rigaud,
Rayol-Canadel 84820.
Tel. 04 94 05 50 06 or 04 94 05 60 30.
A Belle Époque and Art Déco property with a vast park restored with the help of garden designer Gilles Clément (p. 180, 181, 182, 183). Flowers adapted to the mediterranean climate and originating from all five continents are grown.

FONDATION MARGUERITE ET AIMÉ MAEGHT
Musée d'Art moderne et contemporain,
Saint-Paul 06570.
Tel. 04 93 32 81 63.
One of the best contemporary sculpture gardens anywhere features Mirò and Giacometti sculptures and Braque mosaics set among the wind-bent pines.

GALERIE BEAUBOURG
Château Notre-Dame-des-Fleurs, 2618, route de Grasse, Vence 06140.
Tel. 04 93 24 52 00 (reception) or 04 93 24 52 08.
At the foot of a medieval castle and in a terraced garden Marianne and Pierre Nahon display, in front of their Mediterranean gallery of contemporary sculpture, pieces by Niki de Saint-Phalle, Tinguely, Arman, César and others.

GIARDINO BOTANICO HANBURY
La Mortola, 18030 Latte, Italie.
Tel. (39) 0184 229852.
Located on a steep hillside, 2 miles from the Franco-Italian border, the dean of Riviera gardens forms one of the largest Italian experimental gardens which acclimatizes rare and exotic plants. It takes time and concentration to visit but is very much worth the effort. (p. 9, 21, 29, 30-31, 32, 33).

JARDIN BOTANIQUE DE LA VILLE DE NICE
78, Corniche Fleurie, Nice 06200.
Tel. 04 93 71 07 44. Fax. 04 93 71 81 82.
One of the most adventurous public gardens.

JARDIN BOTANIQUE D'ELIE ALEXIS
(Manager: Nicole Manéra)
La Roquebroussane 83136.
Tel. 04 94 86 83 20.
A wonderful garden, home to wild flowers and an exotic garden created by a visionary shepherd.

"JARDIN DES ROMANCIERS" OR FONTANA ROSA
(Owner: Municipality of Menton)
Avenue Blasco-Ibanez, Menton 06500.
Tel. 04 92 10 33 66, Service du Patrimoine de la ville de Menton.
Still in ruins; this garden of Spanish inspiration is full of roses, citrus trees and water. It also possesses numerous and interesting ceramic pieces evoking great literary figures such as Cervantes and Victor Hugo.

GARDEN OF PALAIS CARNOLÈS
(Owner: Menton)
Avenue du Général-de-Gaulle, Menton 06500.
Tel. 04 93 35 49 71.
Set in front of the eighteenth-century art museum built by Jacques Abge Gabriel, this public garden belonging to the town of Menton is home to a collection of approximately fifty different varieties of citrus trees and is laid out formally around two magnificent asymmetric water basins.

JARDIN EXOTIQUE
Eze-Village 06360. Tel. 04 93 41 10 30.
A public garden, at the top of a picturesquely perched village and crowned by the vestiges of an old castle, provides a rich variety of color and sea views over Cap Ferrat, Nice and Antibes. The garden specializes in succulent plants and cacti.

JARDIN EXOTIQUE DE MONACO
(Owner: Principality of Monaco)
Boulevard du Jardin-Exotique, BP 105,
Monaco 98000. Tel. 00 377 93 30 33 65.
Up and down a steep hillside, through grottos and over bridges, one discovers a beautifully designed cactus garden, planted with cacti from Mexico and western Africa. the most visited garden on the Riviera, it receives half a million visitors annually (p. 12).

PARC ST BERNARD
Montée de Noailles, Hyères 83400.
A municipal park overlooking the old town, uniting two very different properties: the Noailles garden famous for its cubist triangle by Gabriel Guévrékian in the Mallet-Stevens villa and the Castel Sainte-Claire restored by Edith Wharton. These public properties are linked by a garden planted with Mediterranean essences.

PARC PHENIX: LE PARC FLORAL DE LA VILLE DE NICE. 405, Promenade des Anglais, Nice 06200. Tel. 04 93 18 03 33 or 04 92 29 33 25.
Situated on the edge of Nice, it stretches across 16 acres. 2500 plant species, 20 themed gardens, and a 7000m² tropical greenhouse.

LA POMME D'AMBRE
(Owner: Mme Nicole Arboireau)
Via Aurélia, La Tour de Mare, Fréjus 83600.
Tel. 04 94 53 25 47. Fax. 04 94 52 95 50.
Pretty garden cared for by a "grandma" who is very knowledgeable when it comes to Mediterranean plants. Open to small groups upon prior request.

"LES COLLETTES" - MAISON DE RENOIR
19, chemin des Collettes, Cagnes-sur-Mer 06800. Tel. 04 93 20 61 07.
Property: The house is owned by the private Fondation Renoir, but the garden is managed by the Commune of Cagnes-sur-Mer and anyone can visit it. The terraces below the charming museum are home to some of the Riviera's most spectacular olive trees. The atmosphere filled with the memory of the painter continues to attract a large number of artists and visitors.

LES COLOMBIÈRES
372, Route de Super Garavan, Menton 06500.
Tel. 04 92 10 33 66
(Service du Patrimoine de la Ville).
Open by appointment only through the municipality of Menton. This is Ferdinand Bac's (painter and garden designer) majestic last and best-known garden. Set in a remarkably protected site, the Mediterranean vegetation, not at all exotic, is organized in a classic fashion by means of astonishing *fabriques* and sculptures. (p.60, 61).

SERRE DE LA MADONE
74, Route du Val de Gorbio, 06500 Menton.
Tel/Fax. 04 93 57 73 90.
This garden was created in the 1920s by Major Lawrence Johnston, to whom we also owe Hidcote in England. It was bought in 1999 by the Conservatoire du Littoral and has been restored by Gilles Clément. It is one of the most beautiful gardens in Europe along with its "twin" garden, Hidcote. (p. 60, 61, 68, 117).

VAL RAHMEH
(Owner: The garden is State owned and is administered by The National Museum of Natural History)
Avenue Saint-Jacques, Menton 06500.
Tel. 04 93 35 86 72 (Tel. 04 92 10 33 66)
This plant collection constitutes the southern branch of The National Museum of Natural History, and is a small but very dense and colorful botanic garden. It houses more than 700 vegetal, woody, or herbaceous species, both local and from across the world: Australia, America or tropical Asia (p.61, 64). Rare cultivated creeper specimens can also be found here, and it is very pleasant to wander in the garden stopping near bowers, fountains and ornamental basins full of water lilies.

VILLA FIESOLE
(Owner: Municipality of Cannes)
19, Impasse Fiesole, Cannes 06400.
Tel. 04 93 68 91 92 (Ask for Mme Zanette on 04 92 98 29 71).
The garden is not open to the public. There is a plan to establish a garden of aromatic plants that would be open along with the villa. For the moment, however, it is only open for official occasions organized by the city of Cannes. Visits are by appointment only and can be arranged with the Service Protocole. (Hôtel de Ville, BP 140, 06406 Cannes Cedex). The painter Jean Gabriel Domergue and sculptor Odette Maugendre-Villers created this elegant domain, with its Italian Renaissance air, so as to host exhibitions, balls and official receptions. It is famous for its dramatic cascade down the hillside (p. 22).

VILLA "ÎLE DE FRANCE"
MUSÉE EPHRUSSI DE ROTHSCHILD
Avenue Ephrussi-de-Rothschild,
Saint-Jean-Cap-Ferrat 06230.
Tel. 04 93 01 33 09.
A series of differently-styled gardens, planted with numerous species, provides the setting for a pink Italianate villa housing fabulous collections which Baroness de Rothschild bequeated to the Institut de France for the Académie des Beaux-Arts (p. 40, 41, 42, 43).

VILLA MARIA SERENA
21, Promenade de la Reine-Astrid, Menton 06500. Tel. 04 92 10 33 66 (Service du Patrimoine de la ville).
Open to groups, which have addressed a written request to the municipality of Menton. A Belle Epoque villa used for receptions, with a hillside of rare specimens of palm trees and brilliantly colorful subtropical plants (p. 13, 25, 65).

VILLA NOAILLES
59, avenue Guy-de-Maupassant, Grasse 06130. Tel. 04 93 36 66 66 (l'Office de tourisme de la ville de Grasse).
Open by appointment for group visits only. A written request in advance is necessary. An Arcadian hillside, full of rare plants and happy harmonies with the creations and acquisitions of the vicomte de Noailles (p. 10, 66 68, 69-70, 72, 73, 77). An impressive collection of camellias in the midst of the olive trees ought to be admired.

VILLA THURET
Chemin G.-Raymond, boulevard du Cap, Antibes 06600.
Tel. 04 93 67 88 00.
These famous botanical gardens belong to the Institut National de Recherche Agronomique. (p. 34). Here G. Thuret introduced subtropical plants which make this one of the oldest collections on the Riviera.

NURSERIES SPECIALIZING
IN MEDITERRANEAN PLANTS

With thanks to Nicole Arboireau and Bruno Goris for their help in establishing this selected list. Although some of these establishments have catalogues, all purchases must be made on the premises.

Specialists in Mediterranean Perennials and Shrubs

ALAIN AYMES & ALAIN MARIE
Chemin du Pas de la chèvre sud, Roc d'Allons-Naron, La Cadière-d'Azur 83740.
Tel. 04 94 32 22 02.
Their lovely display of plants offers more than 3,000 varieties adapted to southern gardens.

BONAUT HORTICULTURE
566, chemin des Maures, Antibes 06600.
Tel. 04 93 33 51 24.
Elie Bonaut and family receive outdoors and in their richly stocked greenhouses. This small family business carefully produces good quality perennials.

PIERRE & MONIQUE CUCHE
Devant-Ville, 83830 Clavier.
Tel. 04 94 76 63 91.
Authors of excellent books on Mediterranean plants and gardens.

PÉPINIÈRES CAVATORE
(Owner: Gérard Cavatore)
Le Mas du Ginget. 488, Chemin de Bénat, 83230 Bormes-les-Mimosas (Acacias).
Wonderful catalogue.

PÉPINIÈRES MICHÈLE DENTAL
1569, route de la Mer, Biot 06470.
Tel. 04 93 65 63 32.
A choice collection of shrubs is entirely produced at the nursery, along with an excellent selection of creepers and rockery plants.

PÉPINIÈRES GAUDISSART
261, chemin des Colles, Vence 06140.
Tel. 04 45 65 02 61.
Director, Pierre Gortina, works closely with designer Jean Mus, providing a good selection of shrubs and groundcovers.

IRIS EN PROVENCE
BP 53, 83402 Hyères cedex.
Tel. 04 94 65 98 30.
Mr. and Mrs. Pierre Anfusso are reputed to have the best European collection of irises.

PÉPINIÈRES DE LA FOUX
781, Chemin de La Foux, Le Pradet 83220.
Tel. 04 94 75 35 45.
Yves Hervé has established here the national collection of sages, among other specialities. He also designs and restores gardens.

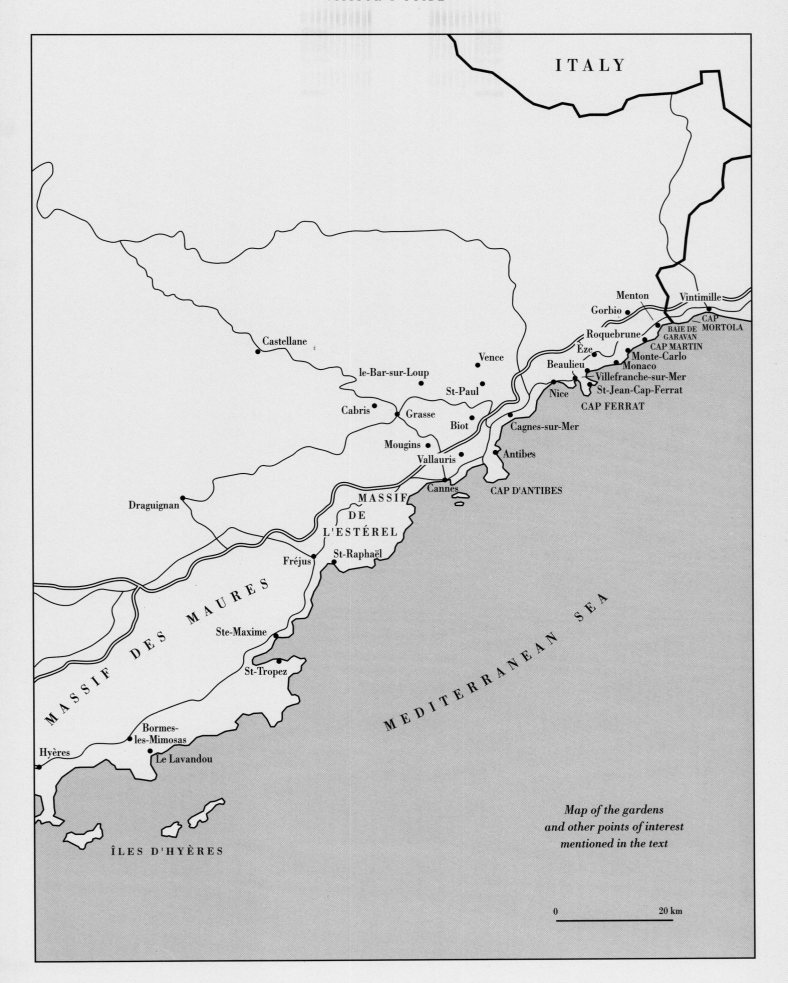

ITALY

Menton · Vintimille

Gorbio ·

CAP MORTOLA

Roquebrune · BAIE DE GARAVAN

CAP MARTIN

Èze · Monte-Carlo

Beaulieu · Monaco

Villefranche-sur-Mer

Nice · St-Jean-Cap-Ferrat

CAP FERRAT

Castellane ·

Vence ·

le-Bar-sur-Loup ·

St-Paul ·

Cabris · Grasse

Biot · Cagnes-sur-Mer

Mougins ·

Vallauris · Antibes

Cannes · CAP D'ANTIBES

Draguignan ·

MASSIF DE L'ESTÉREL

St-Raphaël

Fréjus ·

MASSIF DES MAURES

Ste-Maxime ·

St-Tropez ·

MEDITERRANEAN SEA

Bormes-les-Mimosas ·

Hyères · Le Lavandou ·

ÎLES D'HYÈRES

*Map of the gardens
and other points of interest
mentioned in the text*

0   20 km

PELLIZZARO, DINO
290, chemin de Léouse, Vallauris 06220.
Tel. 04 93 64 18 43.
Dino Pellizzaro, sells rare shrubs and perennials, in particular drought-resistant varieties, and is available for garden design and consultation. He puts out a fascinating catalogue (p. 17, 139, 140).

PÉPINIÈRES REY, JEAN-MARIE
- Jardinerie de Fréjus. Avenue de Provence, Fréjus 83600. Tel. 04 94 52 10 44.
- Route de la Londe-les-Plages, La Londe-les-Maures 83250. Tel. 04 94 66 22 99.
This empire is reputed to be the largest privately-owned nursery in France, supplying many of the smaller ones in the area. It includes a selection of fruit varieties for the south, and disease resistant cypress.

PÉPINIÈRES DE L'ESTÉREL
Route de Bagnols, Fréjus 83600.
Tel. 04 94 51 27 59.
Besides offering his services as a garden consultant, Philippe Miclotte stocks collections of citrus trees, cycads and mimosas, including some very large subjects.

PÉPINIÈRES DU LITTORAL
Route de Roquebrune, Saint-Aygulf 83379.
Tel. 04 94 81 17 17.
Jacques Chupin runs barely 20 acres of nursery, for mainly Mediterranean plants, including varieties for hedging.

SUN PLANTES
Chemin des Couradours, Fréjus 83600.
Tel. 04 94 44 28 67.
Jacques Depiesse deals mainly with professionals but also sells retail. His container plants are carefully nurtured and there is a good choice of climbers.

Cacti

JEAN ARNEODO CACTÉES
603, Chemin du Belvédère, Mougins 06250.
Tel. 04 93 45 05 87.
One of the most appreciated collections.

CACTUS EN PROVENCE
Quartier Saint-Jean, RN 7. Les Arcs 83460.
Tel. 04 94 47 52 24.
Didier Pocreau presents an interesting exhibition of mature plants.

CACTUS ESTÉREL
Chemin de Maupas, Bagnols-en-Forêt, Fréjus 83600. Tel. 04 94 40 66 73.
Another specialist, who offers a large choice for southern gardeners.

ÉTABLISSEMENTS KUENTZ
327, avenue du Général-Brosset, Fréjus 83600.
Tel. 04 94 51 48 66.

Founded in 1907, this is not just a nursery but a park with promenades through succulents of all ages.

PARADIS DES CACTUS
40, avenue Pasteur, Plan-de-Cuques 13380.
Tel. 04 91 68 29 10.
Robert Cerulli cares for 19,500m² of greenhouses and more than 400 varieties of cacti.

Palms and other exotic plants

LES BAMBOUS DE L'HUBAC
Pont de Siagne, Montauroux 83440.
Tel. 04 93 66 12 94.
Benoît Béraud offers some twelve different types of bamboo for sale.

PALMIERS PLANTES EXOTIQUES
766, chemin des Pertuades, Golfe-Juan 06220.
Tel. 04 93 63 68 70.
René Sensi provides a well-presented selection of palms cycads and other exotic plants.

PÉPINIÈRES PALMAZUR
799, chemin Saint-Lazare, Notre-Dame-du-Plan, Hyères 83400. Tel. 04 94 38 91 33.
This is the real specialist in palm varieties, offering many large subjects.

OTHER GARDEN DESIGNERS

BRUNO GORIS
Chemin du Paradis, Gourdon 06620.
Fax. 04 93 42 55 17.
This plant specialist is above all an excellent pratical gardening consultant. (p. 116, 118, 119, 120).

ALAIN GOUDOT, LANDSCAPE ARCHITECT
4, avenue Edmond Salvy, Antibes 06600.
Tel. 04 97 21 70 80. Fax. 04 93 61 99 62. An Artist, historian and designer of avant-garde gardens.

JEAN MUS
Rue Frédéric-Mistral, Cabris 06530.
Tel. 04 93 60 54 50. Fax. 04 93 60 52 81.
The most famous landscapist in the region, Jean Mus, is working on his home ground, which he knows very well. (p. 105, 106, 107, 174, 175).

USEFUL ADDRESSES

LES AMIS DES PARCS ET JARDINS MÉDITERRANÉENS
La Pomme d'Ambre, Via Aurélia, La Tour de Mare, Fréjus 83600. Tel. 04 94 53 25 47.
The goal of this association is to make better known the plants in Mediterranean gardens and parks. Theoretical classes are given and every month a botanical visit is organized in a garden or region. Under its auspices, many exchanges

of seeds and plant cuttings—often quite rare, but always adapted to the region—are made.

ASSOCIATION "FOUS DE PALMIERS"
BP 88, Hyères 83400.
Tel. 04 94 65 85 08 or 04 94 57 67 78.
An association of amateurs and professionals united by the same passion for that exotic tree introduced into France at the end of the last century. The association is interested in everything relevant to the palm tree, from pictorial art representing it, to wines made from it. Visits to gardens with palms in Italy, Portugal and England. Amateurs are given access to specialized libraries and bookshops.

ÉCOLE MÉDITERRANÉENNE DES JARDINS ET DU PAYSAGE
Bastide du Peyrard
BP 62, 06332 Grasse Cedex.
Tel. 04 93 40 47 50.
Professional training and courses.

LA GAZETTE DES JARDINS
(Directeur de publication: Michel Courboulex)
23, avenue du Parc Robiony, Nice 06200.
Tel. 04 93 96 16 13.
The only gardening magazine to give Mediterranean gardens a large coverage.

MEDITERRANEAN GARDEN SOCIETY
Box 14, Peania 19002, Grèce.
Tel. 30 1 801 2741.
Fax. 30 1 623 4105
An intimate but worldwide association that publishes "The Mediterranean Garden", edited by Caroline Harbouri.

SOCIÉTÉ DES GENS DE JARDIN
141, chemin des Maures, Antibes 06600.
Tel. 04 93 95 26 82.
The aim of this association is to incite people to plant species adapted to the local climate in their garden. It hopes to favor the introduction, acclimatization and multiplication of little known plants in France and other European countries. Equally, it tries to sensitize its members not only to the preservation of the existing natural patrimony but also to the improvement of growth and landscaping techniques. It organizes tours of gardens, workshops, and visits to professional horticulturists. The Fête des Plantes at Sofia Antipolis is due to their initiative.

HOTELS AND RESTAURANTS

BASTIDE SAINT-ANTOINE
(Owner and chef: Jacques Chibois)
Rue Henri Dunant, Quartier Saint Antoine, Grasse 06300. Tel. 04 93 70 94 94.
Jacques Chibois offers first rate and original cuisine in one of the best-preserved and most elegant properties near Grasse. The terraced hillside garden provides flowers and herbs for the menu.

GRAND HÔTEL CAP FERRAT
71, bvd. du Général-de-Gaulle, Saint-Jean-Cap-Ferrat 06230. Tel. 04 93 76 50 50.
Wonderful old pines shade a dining terrace overlooking a hillside of brightly colored shrubs. A particularly vibrant, rock garden spreads above the sea-water level swimming pool.

HÔTEL DU CAP-EDEN ROC
Bvd. Kennedy, BP 29, Antibes 06601.
Tel. 04 93 61 39 01.
An immense park, both formal and woodland, leads down to the celebrated restaurant, Eden-Roc, overlooking the sea. This domain, made famous in the 1920s by F. Scott Fitzgerald, is one of the Riviera's best-known luxury hotels.

RESTAURANT MIRAZUR
30, avenue Aristide Briand, 06500 Menton.
Open in the summer 2001.
This is the "bistrot" of the great chef Jacques Chibois from Grasse. Restaured by London architect Rick Mather, its gardens are designed by Arnaud Maurières and Eric Ossart.

MOULIN DE MOUGINS
(Owner and chef: Roger Vergé)
Route de Valbonne, Mougins 06250.
Tel. 04 93 75 78 24.
A series of intimate patio gardens tucked around an old mill add to the charm of this restaurant in which the works of famous contemporary artists (Folon, Arman, César, Fabri...) are on display.

GARDEN DECOR

AUTOUR DE LA TERRE
82, avenue du Maréchal-Juin, Cannes 06400.
Tel. 04 93 43 25 40.
A multitude of items: all kinds of jars, Italian vases, Anduze pottery, a large selection of ancient pottery.

DEMICHELIS
Chemin des Plaines, Mouans-Sartoux 06370.
Tel. 04 93 75 73 73.
This shop will be a joy to lovers of traditional material of local and regional interest, some of which goes back to the eighteenth-century: basins, fountains, tables, benches and more. Contact them directly for more precise information.

FERRONNERIE CHRISTIAN HOOGEWYS
Zone Artisanale, Route de Collobrières, Cogolin 83310. Tel. 04 94 54 13 19.
This master craftsman sells ready- and custom-made metal garden furniture, bringing to his work and all his knowledge and skill. Customers may choose from among many different types of armchairs, consoles, tables and sofas. Christian Hoogewys also makes garden swings, pergolas, belvederes and bowers.

PATRICE HENRY-BIABAUD, POTIER DU JARDIN
Les Vergers, La Garde-Freinet 83680.
Tel. 04 94 43 62 18.
Garden pots and decorative pottery in all shapes and forms.

MAISON JARDIN
2347, avenue du Maréchal-Alphonse-Juin, Mougins 06250. Tel. 04 93 46 29 13.
This manufacturer has a reputation for his love of tradition and authenticity, but at the same time for his ever-renewed sense of creativity. Stone, plaster or terracotta objects are on display and range in size from the monumental to create a transition from house to garden —columns, balustrades—to garden pottery. Maison Jardin stocks a wide selection of vases, window boxes, statues and fountains, which are available in the shop but can also be custom made. Craftsmanship and the inspiration of classical antiquity combine to produce marvelous results.

OBJETS TROUVÉS
1, place des Lices, Sain-Tropez 83990.
Tel. 04 90 20 83 07.
A decoration space dedicated to nature, with a collection of rust-colored iron furniture, wickerwork furniture, and unusually shaped chairs.

PÉPINIÈRES CLÉMENT
(Brigitte or Danièle Clément)
95, avenue de la Buges, Sanary-sur-Mer 83110. Tel. 04 94 74 15 86
A huge choice. Classical pottery, Pronvençal terracotta, glazed and oriental-style vases. Statues, troughs, reconstituted stone. Terracotta pottery from France, Spain, and Italy ranging in style from the simple to the highly ornamental. Opus-Incertum tables in every size, custom made.

POTERIE DES 3 TERRES
Florence and Christian Ploix, BP n°6, Grimaud 83310. Tel. 04 94 43 21 62.
In Grimaud Village, at the heart of Saint-Tropez, the Poterie des 3 Terres has enjoyed an international reputation for over thirty years based on the fine quality of its products. The workshop of Christian and Florence Ploix offers not only a vast choice of hand-painted tiles and house signs but also custom-made garden pottery either simply glazed in white or elaborately decorated in bright colors.

LA POTERIE PROVENÇALE
M. Augé Laribé (fabriquant), 1689, route de la Mer, Biot 06410. Tel. 04 93 65 63 30.
The Augé-Laribé family have been respected potters since the 1920s and are based in an area famous for its clay since prehistoric times. All the great gardens contain d'Augé-Laribé pots.

R. C. B. CARRELAGES
Quartier de la Chaux, Grimaud 83310.
Tel. 04 98 12 60 10.
This huge space is devoted only to the authentic, to terracotta and to tiles, in order to reinforce the character of traditional houses. Objects made of traditional materials are displayed, some of which go back to the eighteenth century (gates, fountains, washtubs, old jars, Anduze vases) as are new creations made according to time-honored methods.

SUN FURNITURE
Galeries du plan, Chez Pépinière Sergui, RD 2085, Roquefort-Les-Pins 06330.
Tel. 04 93 77 00 32.
Hans Wagener represents a large Thai company that specializes in teak furniture which resists weather and age. He offers a large variety of garden and veranda furniture, which ranges from traditional English style to contemporary modern.

TERRE À TERRE
58, avenue Georges-Clemenceau, Vallauris 06220.
Tel. 04 93 63 16 80.
Glazed terracotta jars in different colors.

LA TREILLE MUSCADE
1, place Pellegrini, Nice 06000.
Tel. 04 93 92 15 66.
Old Anduze vases, marbled in the manner traditional to this part of the country.

ALAIN VAGH
Route d'Entrecastreaux, Salernes 83690.
Tel. 04 94 70 61 85.
In this famous workshop in Salernes, one can find natural terracotta or glazed tiles, and outdoor furniture in natural materials.

LA VÉRANDAH
32, quai J.-C. Rey, Monaco 98000.
Tel. 04 92 05 24 01.
Jean-Louis Favre sells all types of furniture: made by craftsmen, classic, in wrought iron— a large selection. He also stocks Tuscan pottery, and more.

GUIDED VISITS
TO RIVIERA GARDENS

BOXWOOD HORTICULTURAL TOURS
in consultation with Louisa Jones
(Director: Mrs. Sue Macdonald)
Llandedr, Gwynedd, LL45 2NT
Wales, UK
Tel. (44) 1 341 241 717
Fax (44) 1 341 241 712
e-mail boxwood@clara.net

Information on visits and agency addresses can be found on the author's web pages: www.enprovence.com/ljones

This list does not include plants common all over Europe unless they are also particularly characteristic of the south, nor does it include collector's items. Chosen here are those plants frequently found in a wide variety of Riviera gardens. Many thanks to specialists Pierre and Monique Cuche for helping draw up the list. It has been cross-checked with the *New Royal Horticultural Society Dictionary of Gardening* (1992) from which most of the English names were taken.

Abutilon megapotamicum, training abutilon, *A. striatum* syn. *A. pictum*, Indian mallow
Acacia baileyana, common wattle, golden mimosa, *A. dealbata*, silver wattle , *A. farnsiana*, mimosa bush, sweet wattle, *A. floribunda*
Acanthus mollis, bear breeches, *A. spinosa*
Aeonium, sp.
Agapanthus umbellatus syn. *A. africanus* and cultivars
Agave, sp. century plant, maguey
Aloe, sp.
Aloysia triphylla syn. *Lippia citrodoria*
Amaryllis belladonna, Jersey lily, bella donna lily
Ampelopsis, sp.
Anemone coronaria and sp.
Anthemis frutescens syn. *Argyranthemum frutescens* syn. *Chrysanthemum frutescens*, dog fennel
Arbutus unedo, strawberry tree
Arctotis, sp. and hybrids
Artemesia, sp., wormwood, sage brush, mugwort
Asphodelus microcarpus syn. *A. aestivus*
Bambusa, sp., bamboo
Beschorneria yuccoides
Bignonia capreolata, cross-vine, quartervine and sp. trumpet flower
Bougainvillea glabra, paper flower, *B. spectabilis*
Brahaea, rock palm, hesper palm
Broussonetia papyrifera, paper mulberry,
Buddleja davidii, *B. madagascariensis*, *B. officinalis*,
Butia capitata, yatay plam, jelly palm
Buxus, box, boxwood ; *B. balearica*, *B. sempervirens*
Cactaceae genera and sp., cactus family
Callistemon sp., bottle-brush
Camellia sp. and cultivars
Campsis radicans, trumpet creeper
Carpobrotus edulis, Hottentot fig
Caryopteris sp. and cultivars, *C. incana*, bluebeard
Cassia sp., golden shower tree, Indian laburnum
Catalpa bignonioides, catawba, Indian bean tree, Indian cigar
Ceanothus sp., California lilac

Cedrus deodora, Himalayan cedar, *C. libani*, cedar of Lebanon, *C. libani* sp. *Atlantica*, Atlas cedar
Celtis australis, nettle tree, hackberry, lotus tree
Ceratostigma larpentae, plumbago, *C. wilmottianum*
Cercis siliquastrum, Judas tree, love tree, redbud
Cestrum aurantiacum, *C. nocturnum*, lady of the night, night jessamine, *C. purpureum*
Chamaerops humilis, dwarf fan palm
Choisya ternara, Mexican orange
Cistus albidus, *C. crispus*, *C. ladanifer*, *C. laurifolius*, *C. parviflorus*, *C. monspeliensis*, *C. salviifolus* and hybrids, cistus, rock-rose
Citrus aurantium, bitter orange, Seville orange *C. limon*, lemon, citronnier, *C. medica*, citron, *C. nobilis*, mandarin, Mandarinier, *C. x paradisi*, pomelo, grape fruit, *C. reticulata*, clementine, satsuma, *C. sinensis*, oranger 'Osbeck' orange
Clematis armandii and cultivars
Clerodendron bungei, glory flower, *C. fragrans* syn. *C. philippinum*, glory bower
Convolvulus cneorum, silverbush, *C. mauritanicus syn. sabatius*
Cordyline australis, *C. indivisa*
Coronilla emerus, scorpion senna, *C. valentina ssp. glauca*
Crinum, sp.
Crocus sativus, saffron and esp.
Cupressus, cypress, *C. lusitanica*, Mexican cypress, Portugese cypress, *C. macrocarpa*, Montereycypress, *C. sempervirens*, Italian cypress
Cycas revoluta, cyad, sago, false sago
Cyclamen, sp.
Cydonia, quince
Cytisus, sp., broom, *C. scoparius* syn. *Genista scoparius*, Spanish broom
Datura arborea syn. *Brugmansia arborea*, thorn apple, *D. candida*, *D. chlorantha* syn. *D. metel*, horn of plenty, downy thorn apple, *D. sanguinea*, *D. suaveolens*, *D. versicolor* and cultivars
Dimorphoteca aurantiaca syn. *D. sinuata*, *D. ecklonis* syn. *Osteospermum ecklonis*, sun marigold
Diospyros, sp. persimmon
Distictis buccinatoria syn. *Phaedranthus buccinatorius*
Dracaena, sp. dragon tree
Echeveria, sp.
Echium fastuosum
Eleagnus, sp., oleaster, silver-berry, Russian olive
Erica arborea, *E. lusitanica*, tree heather
Eriobotrya japonica, Japanese loquat
Erysimum bicolor 'Bowles Mauve', *E. cheiri* syn. *Cheiranthus cheiri*, perennial wallflower

Eucalyptus, sp., gum tree
Euphorbia candelabrum, *E. myrsinites*, *E. resinifera*, spurge
Euryops pectinatus
Exochorda grandiflora syn. *E. racemosa*, pearlbrush
Feijoa sellowiana, pineapple guava
Felicia amelloides, blue daisy
Ficus carica, fig, *F. pumila*, creeping fig
Freesia, sp. and cultivars
Fremontodendron californicum flannel bush, California beauty
Gazania longiscapa syn. *G. linearis*, *G. rigens*, treasure flower
Genista monosperma syn. *Retama monosperma*, broom
Grevillea, sp.
Hebe, esp. and cultivars
Helleborus corsicus, *H. foetidis*, *H. oriental*, *H. niger*, hellebore
Hibiscus rosa-sinensis, *H. syriacus*, hibiscus
Hypericum 'Hidcote'
Ipomoea leari syn. *I. indica*, Blue dawn flower *I. purpura*, common morning glory
Iris germanica, *I. japonica*, *I. unguicularis* syn. *Iris stylosa*, Algerian iris
Jasminum humile, Italian yellow jasmine, *J. officinale*, *J. grandiflorum*, common jasmine, jessamine, polyanthum
Jubaea chilensis, Chilean wine balm
Juniperus, sp.
Koelreuteria paniculata, pride of India, varnish tree, golden rain tree
Lagerstroemia indica, crepe myrtle, Indian lilac
Lampranthus, sp.
Lantana camara, *L. montevidensis* syn. *sellowiana*
Laurus nobilis, sweet bay, bay tree, tree laurel
Lavandula angustifolia syn. *officinalis* syn. *spica* syn. *vera*, English lavender *L. dentata*, *L. latifolia*, *L. stoechas*, French lavender
Lavatera arborea, *L. maritima*, *L. olbia* *L. thuringiaca*, tree lavatera
Leonotis leonurus, lion's ear
Leptospermum lanigerum syn. *pubescens*, ti-tree, tee-tree
Lonicera, sp.
Lotus berthelotii, coral gem
Magnolia grandiflora, large flowered magnolia
Mahonia aquifolium, *M. japonica*, *M. lomariifolia*, Oregon grape, holly grape
Mandevilla laxa syn. *suaveolens*, Chilean jasmine
Melia azederach, China berry, Persian lilac, pride of India, bead tree
Melianthus major, honey flower
Mesembryanthemum, sp., Livingston daisy
Muelhenbeckia complexa maiden hair vine, mattress vine, wire vine
Musa basjoo, Japanese banana *M. x paradisiaca*, edible banana tree

Muscari, sp.

Myrsine africana, Cape myrtle, African boxwood

Myrtus communis, myrtle

Narcissus, sp.

Nerium oleander and cultivars, oleander

Nolina, sp.

Olea europea var. europea, olive

Ornithogalum, sp.

Osteospermum, sp.

Paeonia suffruticosa syn. *arborea* tree peony

Pandorea jasminoides, bower plant, *P. pandorana*, wonga wonga vine

Papyrus, sp.

Parthenocissus, sp.

Passiflora caerulea, P. granadilla syn. edulis, P. quadrangularis, passion flower

Pelargonium, sp. and cultivars

Perovskia atriplicifolia, Russian sage

Phillyrea, sp. *phyllyrea*

Phlomis fruticosa, P. samia, Jersusalem sage

Phoenix canariensis, Canary island date palm

Pinus halepensis, Aleppo pine, *P. pinea*, stone pine, umbrella pine

Pittosporum tenuifolium, P. tobira, mock orange, *P. tobira 'Nana', P. undulatum*, Victorian box

Plumbago auriculata syn. *capensis*, leadwort

Podranea ricasoliana, pink trumpet vine

Polygala myrtifolia

Prunus dulcis, almond

Punica granatum, pomegranate

Quercus coccifera, kermes oak, *Q. ilex*, holm

oak, *Q. suber*, cork oak

Rhamnus, sp. buckthorn

Rhaphiolepis x delacourii, R. indica, R. umbellata

Rhus, sp., sumach

Robinia, sp., acacia

Rosa x anemonoides, R. banksiae 'Lutea', R. chinensis odorata 'Sanguinea', R. chinensis 'General Schablikine', R. indica major, R. laevigata 'La Follette'

Rosmarinus, sp.

Russelia equisetiformis syn. *juncea*

Ruta graveolens : rue, herb of grace

Salvia azurea, S. buchananii, S. elegans, S. greggii, S. guaranitica, S. involucrata, S. leucantha, S. x superba, sage

Santolina, sp., lavender cotton

Sartureia montana, winter savory

Sedum, sp.

Sempervivum, sp.

Schinus molle,

Scilla peruviana and sp.

Senecio cineraria syn. *Cineraria maritima S. grandifolius* syn. *Telanthophora grandifolia, S. greyi* syn. *Brachyglottis greyi, S. petasites*

Solandra maxima syn. *hartwegii, S. grandiflora*

Solanum aviculare, kangaroo apple, *S. jasminoides*, potato vine, *S. rantonettii, S. wendlandii*

Stachys byzantina syn. *lanata*, rabbit ears

Sternbergia lutea

Strelitzia regina

Streptosolen jamesonii, orange browallia, marmalade bush, firebush

Syringa, sp. lilac

Tamarix africana, T. gallica, T. parviflora, T. pentandra

Tecomaria capensis, cape honeysuckle

Tecoma stans

Teucrium fruticans, tree germanda

Thunbergia alata, black-eyed Susan, *T. grandiflora*, blue trumpet vine

Thymus, sp., thym

Trachelospermum jasminoides syn. *Rhynchospermum jasminoides*, star jasmine, jessamine

Tropaeolum, sp.

Tulipa, sp., tulip

Urginea maritima, sea onion

Verbena, sp. and hybrids

Veronica, sp.

Viburnum tinus

Vitis, sp. and hybrids

Vittidinia triloba syn. *Erigeron karvinskianus* syn. *E. mucronatus*

Vitex agnus castus, cactus snail tree

Washingtonia filifera, palm

Wisteria, W. floribunda, W. japonica, W. sinenis

Zantedeschia aethiopia, arum lily

Zizyphus jujuba, common jujube, Chinese date

B I B L I O G R A P H Y

GARDEN HISTORY

ARBOIREAU, Nicole, *Jardins de grands-mères*, Edisud, Aix-en-Provence, 1999.

BOURSIER-MOUGENOT, Ernest J.-P. et RACINE Michel, *Jardins de la Côte d'Azur*, Edisud Arpej, Aix-en-Provence, 1987.

BYK, Christian, *Guide des jardins de Provence et de Côte d'Azur*, Editions Berger Levrault-Nice Matin, Paris, 1988.

CAMERON, Roderick, *The Golden Riviera*, Editions Limited, Honolulu, 1975.

DEJEAN-ARRECGROS, J., *Les Itinéraires fleuris de la Côte d'Azur*, Delachaux et Niestlé, Neuchâtel, 1980.

CASTRIES, duc de, *Merveilles des châteaux de Provence*, Hachette, Paris, 1965.

FORTESCUE, Winifred, *Perfume from Provence*, William Blackwood and Sons, Edinburgh, 1950.

LEGRAIN, Dominique, *Le Conservatoire du Littoral*, Actes Sud / Editions locales de France, 2000.

MOSSER, Monique and Teyssot, Georges, *Histoire des jardins de la Renaissance à nos jours*, Flammarion, Paris, 1991.

QUEST-RITSON, Charles, *The English Garden Abroad*, Viking, London, 1992.

Rose, Rosa, Rosae, catalogue d'exposition, Musée international de la parfumerie, Grasse, 1991.

RUSSELL, Vivian, *Gardens of the Riviera*, Little Brown and Co., London, 1993.

VALÉRY, Marie-Françoise and LÉVEQUE, Georges, *French Garden Style*, Francis Lincoln, Londres, 1991.

ZUYLEN, Gabrielle van, and PEREIRE, Anita, *Jardins privés de France*, Arthaud, Paris, 1983.

ZUYLEN, Gabrielle van and SCHINZ, Marina, *The Gardens of Russell Page*, Stewart, Tabori and Chang, New York, 1992.

PRATICAL WORKS

BECKER, M. PICARD, J.-F., TIMBAL, J., *Je reconnais les arbres, arbustes et abrisseaux : région méditerranéenne*, André Leson, Paris, s. d.

CHIBOIS, Jacques et BAUSSAN, Olivier, *Saveurs et parfums de l'huile d'olive*, Flammarion, Paris, 1999.

CRUSE, Éléonore, *Roses anciennes et botaniques*, Éditions du Chêne, Paris, 1997.

CUCHE, Pierre and Monique, *Jardins du Midi : L'Art et la Manière*, Edisud, Aix-en-Provence, 1997.

Cuche, Pierre and Monique, *Plantes du Midi*, 2 vol., Edisud, Aix-en-Provence, 1999.

DEJEAN-ARRECGROS, J., *Comment aménager son jardin en Provence et sur la Côte d'Azur*, Solar, Paris, 1982.

DELANGE, Yves, *Les Fleurs des jardins méditeranéens*, Larousse, Paris, 1991.

DELANGE, Yves, *Le jardin familial méridional*, Paris, La Maison Rustique, 1980.

DELANGE, Yves, *Les Végétaux des milieux arides*, Editions du Rocher, Paris, 1992.

GILDEMEISTER, Heidi, *Votre Jardin méditerranéen*, Edisud, Aix-en-Provence, 1996.

GIUGLARIS, August Louis, *De l'acclimatation des végétaux dans le Midi de la France*, Société générale de l'imprimerie, Nice, 1940.

HARANT, H., et JARRY, D., *Guide du naturaliste dans le Midi de la France*, Delachaux et Niestlé, Neuchâtel, 1967, 2 volumes.

HAUDEBOURG, Marie-Thérèse, *Roses et Jardins*, Hachette, Paris, 1995.

HUXLEY, Anthony, sous la direction de, The New Royal Horticultural Society *Dictionary of Gardening*, Macmillan, London, 1992, 4 volumes.

JONES, Louisa, *L'Année jardinière en Provence*, Edisud, Aix-en-Provence, 1999.

JONES, Louisa, *L'Esprit nouveau des jardins : un art, un savoir vivre en Provence*, Hachette, Livres pratiques, Paris, 1998.

LATYMER, Hugo, *The Mediterranean Gardener*, Frances Lincoln, London, 1990.

MAURIÈRES, Arnaud and Rey, Jean-Marie, *Le Jardinier de Provence et des régions méditerranéennes*, Edisud, Aix-en-Provence, 1995.

MENZIES, Yve, *Mediterranean Gardening : a Practical Handbook*, John Murray, London, 1991.

MUS, Jean, *Les Jardins de Provence*, Éditions du Chêne, Paris, 1996.

NOAILLES, vicomte de et LANCASTER, Roy, *Plantes de jardins méditerranéens*, Larousse, Paris, 1977.

PHILLIPS, Roger, *Fleurs de Méditerranée*, Bordas, Paris, s. d.

POLUNIN, Oleg and Huxley, Anthony, *Flowers of the Mediterranean*, The Hogarth Press, London, 1987.

I N D E X